T0295616

Managing Decline

A growing body of literature in the area of business administration has focused on the phenomenon of decline. These studies span multiple levels of analysis and draws on a range of disciplines, including strategic management, economics, and economic geography.

Managing Decline: A Research Overview provides a summary of this research by focusing on three key levels of analysis: industries, clusters, and organizations. The targeted reviews in this book map each individual level of analysis separately and the discussion section outlines overarching themes regarding decline and its management. The three levels are analyzed by identifying different forms, causes, processes, and management options regarding decline. This is accompanied by the identification of key academic discourses that have been used to analyze decline. The discussion section highlights broader themes regarding the nature and management of decline that span across the different levels of analysis.

This book provides an easy-to-access summary on the nature and management of decline for academic scholars and business practitioners, and is essential reading for getting an overview of this broad field of research.

Antti Sihvonen is Lecturer in Strategy and Entrepreneurship at Jyväskylä University School of Business and Economics, Finland.

Juha-Antti Lamberg is Professor of Strategy and Economic History at the University of Jyväskylä, Finland.

Henrikki Tikkanen is A. I. Virtanen Professor of Consumer Research at Aalto University School of Business, Finland.

State of the Art in Business Research
Series Editor: Geoffrey Wood

Recent advances in theory, methods and applied knowledge (alongside structural changes in the global economic ecosystem) have presented researchers with challenges in seeking to stay abreast of their fields and navigate new scholarly terrains.

State of the Art in Business Research presents short-form books which provide an expert map to guide readers through new and rapidly evolving areas of research. Each title will provide an overview of the area, a guide to the key literature and theories and time-saving summaries of how theory interacts with practice.

As a collection, these books provide a library of theoretical and conceptual insights, and exposure to novel research tools and applied knowledge, that aid and facilitate in defining the state of the art, as a foundation stone for a new generation of research.

Philosophy and Management Studies
A Research Overview
Raza Mir and Michelle Greenwood

Work in the Gig Economy
A Research Overview
James Duggan, Anthony McDonnell, Ultan Sherman and Ronan Carbery

Organizing Corporeal Ethics
A Research Overview
Alison Pullen and Carl Rhodes

Managing Decline
A Research Overview
Antti Sihvonen, Juha-Antti Lamberg and Henrikki Tikkanen

For more information about this series, please visit: www.routledge.com/State-of-the-Art-in-Business-Research/book-series/START

Managing Decline

A Research Overview

Antti Sihvonen, Juha-Antti Lamberg, and Henrikki Tikkanen

Routledge
Taylor & Francis Group

LONDON AND NEW YORK

First published 2022
by Routledge
2 Park Square, Milton Park, Abingdon, Oxon OX14 4RN

and by Routledge
605 Third Avenue, New York, NY 10158

Routledge is an imprint of the Taylor & Francis Group, an informa business

© 2022 Antti Sihvonen, Juha-Antti Lamberg and Henrikki Tikkanen

The right of Antti Sihvonen, Juha-Antti Lamberg and Henrikki Tikkanen
to be identified as authors of this work has been asserted in accordance
with sections 77 and 78 of the Copyright, Designs and Patents Act 1988.

Trademark notice: Product or corporate names may be trademarks or
registered trademarks, and are used only for identification and explanation
without intent to infringe.

British Library Cataloguing-in-Publication Data
A catalogue record for this book is available from the British Library

Library of Congress Cataloging-in-Publication Data
Names: Sihvonen, Antti, 1983– author. | Lamberg, Juha-Antti, author. |
    Tikkanen, Henrikki, author.
Title: Managing decline : a research overview / Antti Sihvonen, Juha-Antti
    Lamberg and Henrikki Tikkanen.
Description: Abingdon, Oxon ; New York, NY : Routledge, 2022. | Series:
    State of the art in business research | Includes bibliographical
    references and index.
Identifiers: LCCN 2021038539 (print) | LCCN 2021038540 (ebook) |
    ISBN 9780367900298 (hbk) | ISBN 9781032192901 (pbk) |
    ISBN 9781003035947 (ebk)
Subjects: LCSH: Business—Research. | Management—Research.
Classification: LCC HD30.4 .S54 2022 (print) | LCC HD30.4 (ebook) |
    DDC 650.072—dc23/eng/20211005
LC record available at https://lccn.loc.gov/2021038539
LC ebook record available at https://lccn.loc.gov/2021038540

ISBN: 978-0-367-90029-8 (hbk)
ISBN: 978-1-032-19290-1 (pbk)
ISBN: 978-1-003-03594-7 (ebk)

DOI: 10.4324/9781003035947

Typeset in Times New Roman
by Apex CoVantage, LLC

Contents

Figures

Acknowledgements

The authors wish to thank the "Crises Redefined: Historical Continuity and Societal Change" and "Learning from the past for the future: A historical perspective on industrial and strategic change" projects financed by the Academy of Finland and the Marcus Wallenberg Foundation for their support in the preparation of this book. The authors would also like to thank Nooa Nykänen and Mirva Peltoniemi on their helpful comments on the manuscript.

1 Introduction

Prolegomena to decline as a phenomenon

When we started brainstorming about this book in the early summer of 2019, one of the authors noted that the topic is not very timely, but it will become when the economy hits the next speedbump and trouble starts. A year later, in the fall of 2020, this book was written and discussions of decline have become ubiquitous as the Covid-19 pandemic has ravaged the global economy. We do not tell this anecdote to indicate that we were prescient, but rather to explain how decline is generally approached. Nobody wants to think about it until it happens.

Organizational decline, the dark underbelly of success, is shrugged off as the natural detritus of economic and technological progress, a nuisance generated by economic cycles, an outcome of mismanagement, or the consequence of unexpected events that no one can control. In doing so, analyses of decline are easily kept from the popular press and our general consciousness until organizational decline and failure come knocking. For instance, rarely do people talk about the industries and companies that have failed.

A similar tendency is reflected in the definition of *decline*. The dictionaries offer the following definitions:

> "to gradually become less, worse, or lower: . . .
> when something becomes less in amount, importance, quality, or strength: . . .
> a change to a lower amount; the process of becoming less in quality or strength: . . .
> to become less, worse, or lower in value: . . .
> to make less profit, or produce less: . . ." (Cambridge dictionary)[1]
> "1: to become less in amount . . .
> 2: to tend toward an inferior state or weaker condition . . .
> 6 archaic: to turn from a straight course . . ." (Merriam-Webster)[2]

DOI: 10.4324/9781003035947-1

Based on these definitions, decline can be understood as the moment when something becomes worse, when its value deteriorates, or when it becomes less important. Embedded in these meanings is the idea that decline is a downward deviation from the normal course of events. Therefore, it is no surprise that decline in our everyday parlance is associated with a loss of importance.

Our point is that decline is presumably negative. While we may prefer not to think about decline, it is a natural economic process. Therefore, whether in the midst of a crisis or not, we should understand what decline means for organizations, economic clusters, and industries, and why and how it affects their functioning. Moreover, a key question is how – if at all – decline can be managed. This is the theme of our book.

Curating a review on decline

While a pedestrian reading of the term *decline* sparks little excitement, academic research in business administration is no stranger to the concept. Many papers have studied decline from different theoretical perspectives and at different levels of economic activity. Therefore, we limit our inquiry to three overlapping levels of analysis: *industry*, *cluster*, and *company*. Figure 1.1 offers the initial working definitions for each of these analytical levels to prepare the reader for the content of our treatise. The decision to focus on these three levels of analysis is based on the amount of research that has focused on each of them and their nearness to (strategic) management as an academic and practical discipline. These levels overlap because companies,

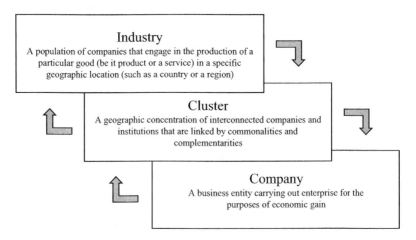

Industry
A population of companies that engage in the production of a particular good (be it product or a service) in a specific geographic location (such as a country or a region)

Cluster
A geographic concentration of interconnected companies and institutions that are linked by commonalities and complementarities

Company
A business entity carrying out enterprise for the purposes of economic gain

Figure 1.1 Levels of analysis

other organizations, and their key decision-makers are the primary actors. However, the levels above the industry and cluster levels are more than mere aggregations of lower-level activity since they can act as important meso- and macro-level actors in their own right (e.g., Hillman 1982; Klepper 1997; Martin and Sunley 2003).

Given the myriad of decline studies, why is another book on the topic needed? Our answer is threefold. We begin with a summary of the literature on the decline of industries, clusters, and companies to highlight the central academic discourses on decline and failure. In doing so, this book is the first to compile the research on the three analytical levels. We therefore contend that this book offers both researchers and managers an overview on how decline has been studied. Since our review is by no means the first survey of the literature on each level of analysis, we complement our analysis by identifying key meta-analyses and reviewing studies that provide further insight into each level of analysis.

In addition, we examine decline across the three levels of analysis to arrive at new conclusions about decline and how it can be managed. The research to date has focused on a single level of analysis (e.g., Mellahi and Wilkinson 2004; Lamberg, Ojala and Peltoniemi 2018). Many of the studies are also limited by the constraints of academic journals that preclude the multilevel analysis of decline. We therefore hope that this book can show researchers how different levels of analysis might be connected and what other avenues for further research there might be.

Finally, we outline how decline can be managed on and across all levels of analysis. Our review gathers accessible managerial insights into diagnosing decline and pinpointing ways of managing it. We hope that practicing managers will find that this book helps them to understand what they can do at the worst of times.

We answer four research questions in our analysis of decline. This is crucial because we lack a uniform discourse(s) that spans all levels of analysis. By answering these questions, we hope to put together the puzzle of industry, cluster, and organizational decline and failure. These questions are:

1   *What constitutes decline?*
2   *What causes decline?*
3   *What happens during decline?*
4   *How can decline be managed?*

By analyzing each level of decline, we have a natural entry point to understanding it. This helps us delineate what decline means in different contexts and from different theoretical angles. Each chapter begins with a definition. Thereafter, by analyzing the causes of decline, we give the reader an understanding of what factors can set an industry, a cluster, or a company on a trajectory of decline and eventual failure. This analysis suggests an array of precursors that can be used to diagnose the causes of decline. When decline does take place, we analyze the forms it can take and the dynamics of different processes of decline. This showcases what different actors do when decline happens and how their actions can either fend off or accelerate decline. Finally, building on the causes and forms of decline, we analyze how decline can be managed by presenting the readers with a variety of options. We hope to demonstrate that companies have options other than ossification when decline happens and that there are ways to survive and even thrive despite adverse conditions.

Overview of the chapters

Our review consists of four chapters. Each of the first three chapters concentrates on a single level of analysis, while the final chapter draws together unifying themes. The following section introduces the content of each chapter.

Chapter 2 begins with an analysis of industry decline. What cuts across this analysis is the distinction between continuous and discontinuous decline and how it affects the causes and processes of decline. In our analysis, we foreground the importance of key strands of literature that have influenced this field. These strands include population ecology (Hannan and Freeman 1977; Ruef 2004), industry life-cycle theory (e.g., Klepper 1997; Peltoniemi 2011), and the literature on business exits (Ghemawat and Nalebuff 1985, 1990).

In Chapter 3, we home in on industry clusters. We discuss cluster evolution and links to adjacent discussions, especially in economic geography. Cluster decline appears as the loss of competitiveness and an inability to renew the cluster. Thereafter, the chapter looks for factors and processes that the literature has found to have a causal impact on cluster decline. Factors such as labor or natural resources and processes such as lock-in, globalization, or an exit of an anchor firm cut across the literatures in economic geography (e.g., Menzel and Fornahl 2010; Hassink 2016), strategic management (Jacobides and Tae 2015; Teece 2007), and business history (Amdam and Bjarnar 2015; Parsons and Rose 2005).

In Chapter 4 we turn to individual companies. The chapter highlights organizational failure as the most often-used label for organizational decline and these labels are therefore used interchangeably. The chapter then presents the deterministic, voluntaristic, and entrepreneurial perspectives to organizational decline and failure that have been foregrounded as the central approaches for the study of organizational failure (Kücher and Feldbauer-Durstmüller 2019; Mellahi and Wilkinson 2004). These perspectives provide different insights into the causes, processes, and management of organizational decline.

Finally, in Chapter 5 we focus on the management of decline across the three levels of analysis. This analysis is divided into two parts. The first part discusses key themes and observations in the different levels of analysis. These themes relate to the nature and causes of decline, relationships between different levels of analysis, and the outcomes of decline. The second part discusses four archetypal approaches to the management of decline, ranging from preventive actions to structural changes and letting go at the point of no return.

Notes

1 https://dictionary.cambridge.org/dictionary/english/decline
2 www.merriam-webster.com/dictionary/decline

References

Amdam, R. P., & Bjarnar, O. (2015). Globalization and the development of industrial clusters: Comparing two Norwegian clusters, 1900–2010. *Business History Review, 89*(4), 693–413. https://doi.org/10.1017/S0007680515001051

Ghemawat, P., & Nalebuff, B. (1985). Exit. *The RAND Journal of Economics, 16*(2), 184–194.

Ghemawat, P., & Nalebuff, B. (1990). The devolution of declining industries. *The Quarterly Journal of Economics, 105*(1), 167–186. https://doi.org/10.2307/2937824

Hannan, M. T., & Freeman, J. (1977). The population ecology of organizations. *American Journal of Sociology, 82*(5), 929–964. https://doi.org/10.1086/226424

Hassink, R. (2016). Cluster decline and political lock-ins. In Fiorenza Belussi & Jose Luis Hervás-Oliver (Eds.), *Unfolding Cluster Evolution*. London: Routledge.

Hillman, A. L. (1982). Declining industries and political-support protectionist motives. *The American Economic Review, 72*(5), 1180–1187.

Jacobides, M. G., & Tae, C. J. (2015). Kingpins, bottlenecks, and value dynamics along a sector. *Organization Science, 26*(3), 889–907. https://doi.org/10.1287/orsc.2014.0958

Klepper, S. (1997). Industry life cycles. *Industrial and Corporate Change, 6*(1), 145–182. https://doi.org/10.1093/icc/6.1.145

Kücher, A., & Feldbauer-Durstmüller, B. (2019) Organizational failure and decline – A bibliometric study of the scientific frontend. *Journal of Business Research, 98*, 503–516. https://doi.org/10.1016/j.jbusres.2018.05.017

Lamberg, J. A., Ojala, J., & Peltoniemi, M. (2018). Thinking about industry decline: A qualitative meta-analysis and future research directions. *Business History, 60*(2), 127–156. https://doi.org/10.1080/00076791.2017.1340943

Martin, R., & Sunley, P. (2003). Deconstructing clusters: Chaotic concept or policy panacea? *Journal of Economic Geography, 3*(1), 5–35. https://doi.org/10.1093/jeg/3.1.5

Mellahi, K., & Wilkinson, A. (2004). Organizational failure: A critique of recent research and a proposed integrative framework. *International Journal of Management Reviews, 5–6*(1), 21–41. https://doi.org/10.1111/j.1460-8545.2004.00095.x

Menzel, M. P., & Fornahl, D. (2010). Cluster life cycles – Dimensions and rationales of cluster evolution. *Industrial and Corporate Change, 19*(1), 205–238. https://doi.org/10.1093/icc/dtp036

Parsons, M., & Rose, M. B. (2005). The neglected legacy of Lancashire cotton: Industrial clusters and the U.K. outdoor trade, 1960–1990. *Enterprise and Society, 6*(4), 682–709. https://doi.org/10.1017/s1467222700015299

Peltoniemi, M. (2011). Reviewing industry life-cycle theory: Avenues for future research. *International Journal of Management Reviews, 13*(4), 349–375. https://doi.org/10.1111/j.1468-2370.2010.00295.x

Ruef, M. (2004). For whom the bell tolls: Ecological perspectives on industrial decline and resurgence. *Industrial and Corporate Change, 13*(1), 61–89. https://doi.org/10.1093/icc/13.1.61

Teece, D. J. (2007). Explicating dynamic capabilities: The nature and microfoundations of (sustainable) enterprise performance. *Strategic Management Journal, 28*(13), 1319–1350. https://doi.org/10.1002/smj.640

2 Understanding declining industries and management during decline

What constitutes industry decline

To provide an overview of research on the topic of industry decline, we must first expand upon what constitutes 'industry' and 'decline' in the literature. Although it has rarely been defined, industry is generally understood as a population of companies that engage in the production of a product or service in a specific geographic location (such as a country or a region). This is how Lamberg, Ojala and Peltoniemi (2018) define industry in their meta-analysis of industry decline. It is also reflected in the case studies of industry decline in the US automotive industry (Fasenfest and Jacobs 2003; Freedman and Blair 2010), British production industries in general (Donnelly, Begley and Collis 2017; McCloskey 1973; McGovern 2011) and especially its textile industry (Filatotchev and Toms 2003; Higgins and Toms 2003; Lazonick 1981, 1983; Porac, Thomas and Baden-Fuller 2011). In doing so, a large body of literature on decline has analyzed how certain industries in different countries wither over time. This implies that decline is a location-specific phenomenon. Decline is also rarely a terminal state for a local industry since some remnants usually remain even if most of companies cease to exist and industry output plunges. This has been the case, for instance, with the Mexican oil industry (Haber, Maurer and Razo 2003), the Japanese coal industry (Garside 2005), and the European fertilizer industry (Lie 2008).

In addition to permanent decay, decline also encompasses shocks that can temporarily send industries into decline or radically alter their operation. These shocks are becoming more commonplace due to the increased globalization of industries and result from events such as the global financial crisis of 2007 (Huhtala et al. 2014; Lai 2010) or the Covid-19 pandemic of 2020 (Hitt, Arregle and Holmes 2021; Rouleau, Hällgren and de Rond 2021). In this chapter we examine both continuous and discontinuous decline and elaborate this distinction in the sections that analyze different forms of decline and their management.

DOI: 10.4324/9781003035947-2

To examine what constitutes industry decline, it is logical to ask how we can know that an industry has entered a phase of decline. Researchers have used numerous most-often quantitative indicators to ascertain that an industry is indeed in decline. These indicators can be grouped into three classes. Table 1.1 provides an overview of these classes, outlines indicators belonging to each class, and identifies exemplary studies that belong to each class.

The first class, *decline in industry output and size*, covers indicators related to a decrease in the output or capacity of an industry, decline in the

Table 1.1 Different classes of industry decline, their indicators, and exemplary studies

Classes of decline	Indicators of decline	Exemplary studies
Decline in industry output and size	Decline in output or capacity of an industry	Dinlersoz and MacDonald (2009), Donnelly, Begley and Collis (2017), Garside (2005), Lie (2008), Lieberman (1990), Slade (2015)
	Decline in the number of companies	Dinlersoz and MacDonald (2009), Lie (2008), Ruef (2004)
	Decline in the number of jobs	Cassing and Hillman (1986), Garside (2005), Kalafsky and MacPherson (2002), Fasenfest and Jacobs (2003)
Market decline	Decline in sales	Chandler, Broberg and Allison (2014), Filatotchev and Toms (2003), Miles, Snow and Sharfman (1993), Morrow, Johnson and Busenitz (2004)
	Decline in demand	Anand and Singh (1997), Ghemawat and Nalebuff (1990), Harrigan and Porter (1983), Takahashi (2015)
	Decline in market share	Bakker (2005), Freedman and Blair (2010)
Decline in industry renewal	Decline in innovation and patents	Arora, Branstetter and Drev (2013), Chatterji and Fabrizio (2016)
	Decline of investments	Slade (2015)

number of companies, and decline in the number of jobs in an industry. As an example of this kind of decline, Garside (2005) traced the decline of Japan's coal industry though the closure of production units and loss of jobs. This type of decline can be directly observed from the size of the industry in a country or region.

The second class is *market decline*. Here deterioration can be observed from the decreasing sales of an industry, withering demand for an industry's output, or decreasing global market share of an industry. In this type of decline, an industry is facing a permanent decline either due to changes in customer behavior or through inability to compete against other industries or global players in their own industry. Competition with other industries relates to the price competition and industries' capacity to fulfill customer need better than their competitors. In their study of market decline, Filatotchev and Toms (2003) recount how the UK cotton textile industry deteriorated due to loss of sales to foreign competitors that entered the UK market while losing position in export markets.

The third and final class is a *decline in industry renewal*. This is manifested in the decrease in innovation and meager number of patents that an industry produces, or in the lack of investments that would renew the industry. All of these factors undermine the capacity of an industry stay competitive. Arora, Branstetter and Drev (2013) attributed the decline of the Japanese information technology (IT) industry to a decline in innovation and patenting in comparison to American IT industry.

Taken together, these three classes cover many of the common indicators that researchers have used to diagnose an industry in decline. However, there is substantial diversity in what is perceived to constitute decline; many studies see decline in a combination of factors since different classes of decline are linked. What is also noteworthy is that what studies conceive as decline and how decline is measured is linked to the causes of decline and the form of decline facing an industry. Thus, next we will focus on what causes industries to decline.

What causes industry decline

Our analysis of the literature revealed more than 20 causes of industry decline. To formulate a coherent picture of what causes industry decline, we aggregated these causes into six categories: *customer behavior, innovation, market dynamics, industry maturity, legislation and policy*, and *exogenous events* (Figure 2.1). The categories share similarities with the causes identified by Lamberg, Ojala and Peltoniemi (2018) in their meta-analysis of historical studies on decline, not least because our analysis covers many of the same studies.[1] We now unpack the causes one by one.

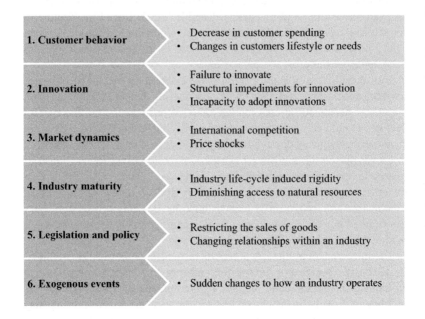

Figure 2.1 Causes of industry decline

Customer behavior

Changes in customer behavior can decrease demand for an industry's goods (Anand and Singh 1997; Harrigan and Porter 1983; McGovern 2011). Customer behavior is often treated as an exogenous change that is actualized either through decreases in customer spending or through changes in customer lifestyle or needs. These changes can be difficult for an industry to address, leading to a diminishing market and eventually a state of decline.

A decrease in customer spending is often cited as a manifestation of challenges that customers face which influences their wellbeing and willingness to buy. In doing so, the digitalization of retailing negatively influenced the retail fixture industry that depended on sales to brick-and-mortar stores (Chandler, Broberg and Allison 2014). Similarly, the declining number of British car producers directly influenced the demand that the British tire industry had in supplying car producers with tires for new vehicles (McGovern 2011). Thus, changes in the structure and health of customer industries can seep up the value chain and induce decline in the supplier industries.

In addition to a decrease in customer spending, decline can be caused by changes in customer lifestyle or needs (e.g., Chandler, Broberg and Allison

2014; Harrigan and Porter 1983; Garside 2005). Here customer lifestyles and needs are understood to emerge from consumers' income, age, ethnicity, and lifestyle choices that generate a plethora of market segments that a company can target (Sheth and Sisodia 1999). While some of these changes occur within a product category and could be addressed through increased innovation and product development, customers also switch to new product categories. Meeting those needs can be beyond the reach of established industries. As examples, Freedman and Blair (2010) attribute the decline of the US auto industry to a general inability to understand customers' need for smaller and more fuel-efficient cars that Japanese producers were able to supply. Takahashi (2015) recounts how the US movie theater industry faced an insurmountable challenge during the 1950s when televisions replaced movie theaters as the main channel of media consumption. In both studies, the cause of decline can be traced to changes in customer needs but the possibility for an industry to address these changes differed. Changes in customer behavior can therefore send an industry into a market decline as demand or customer spending enters a slump.

Innovation

Innovation and technological development change the competitive landscape and send industries that are unable to innovate or follow technological development into decline. In this regard, the comparison of the US and Japanese IT industries by Arora, Branstetter and Drev (2013) is highly instructive. Their study revealed how the decline of Japanese IT industry was largely due to the incapacity to innovate in the software domain as the focus of the global IT industry changed from hardware to software. This transition enabled the American IT industry to dominate the global IT industry. The emergence of new technologies also leads to technological displacement, where industries that rely on older technologies become displaced by those that have adopted newer and more advanced technologies (Adner and Snow 2010).

Beyond superficial explanations of the lack of innovation, industries may face more deep-seated structural impediments to innovation. Freedman and Blair (2010) argued that in the 1970s and 1980s, American automakers were unable to develop the small and fuel-efficient cars that customers demanded. While changing customer needs are often a central reason for industry decline, a major impediment to addressing customer needs was US automakers' heavy focus on efficiency. This hampered their capacity to adapt to changes and to develop new car models that were suited to customers' lifestyles and needs.

Structural reasons also extend to the adoption of innovation. Here Lazonick's (1981, 1983) analyses of the British cotton industry are highly influential. What Lazonick found was that even though British textile machinery companies developed and manufactured advanced production machinery, these innovations were not adopted by the textile production industry because it would have necessitated the integration of spinning and weaving that were done by separate specialized companies. This separation was ingrained in managers' mindset of how the industry operates and led the once-dominant British cotton industry to become technologically backward.

While the failure to innovate is an often-cited cause for decline, explanations of these failures are often grounded in other industry-related factors that decrease the innovation performance of an industry and cause a decline in industry renewal.

Market dynamics

Among the known causes for industry decline, market dynamics is the most commonly inferred. As Lamberg, Ojala and Peltoniemi (2018) have noted:

> The literature on industry decline concentrates almost entirely on one or more countries (such as Europe or the British empire) competing in international markets. Therefore, competitiveness in the global market is either taken for granted or viewed as a trigger for decline, although the primary causes of decline might arguably be found elsewhere (such as in institutions, technology, or capabilities).
>
> (pp. 135–136)

This tendency is also reflected in our analysis since competition with foreign industries is often identified as the overarching cause of decline.

International competition can undermine industries on at least two fronts. Increased imports decrease the market share that a local industry has in its home market (Fasenfest and Jacobs 2003; Kalafsky and MacPherson 2002; Lie 2008; Porac, Thomas and Baden-Fuller 2011). This inevitably leads to the displacement of a local industry with foreign imports. In addition, losing global competitiveness decreases the exports of a local industry and undermines its prospects (e.g., Amankwah-Amoah 2015; Donnelly, Begley and Collis 2017). This kind of decline can be especially tricky for industries in which many companies are owned by multinational corporations. The inability to generate scale economies, to benefit from the concentration of multiple actor groups, and to assume high enough profitability make it challenging to justify keeping production in low-productivity countries when it can be moved to lower-cost countries. The analysis of the West Midland automotive industry by Donnelly, Begley and Collis (2017) is a fitting example. Local industries also often experience a double blow from these factors when the local market is gnawed away by cheap imports, while the industry struggles to export its goods. For instance, the UK cotton textile industry deteriorated as a result of import penetration and simultaneous loss of exports (Filatotchev and Toms 2003).

In addition to locating the cause of decline in the competitiveness of an industry vis-à-vis its rivals, price shocks and decreases in the price of an industry's output have been noted as another cause of decline. Examining this cause is especially pertinent in economics, where studies have scrutinized how import tariffs can influence and potentially forestall the decline of an industry that faces decreasing prices (Brainard and Verdier 1997; Cassing and Hillman 1986; Hillman 1982). Hillman (1982) explains this logic of decline by noting that a fall in the world price of an industry's output directly incurs income losses to a declining industry since industry-specific factors cannot be assigned to other more productive purposes. We can therefore conclude that market dynamics are often responsible for steering an industry into a market decline.

Industry maturity

Industry maturity and development of an industry can also sow the seeds of decline. In this regard, industry life cycle is an often-cited cause for decline (Baptista and Karaöz 2011; Dinlersoz and MacDonald 2009; Karniouchina et al. 2013; Morrow, Johnson and Busenitz 2004). The early stages of an industry life cycle are marked by a variety in product innovation and entry of new companies (Klepper 1997; see also Peltoniemi 2011) that enable industries to adapt to environmental changes. However, as an industry grows and matures, the focus shifts to process R&D and scale economies. Simultaneously, the number of firms in an industry drops when it becomes dominated by a few large companies whose size gives them an advantage. This diminishes the variety of competitive strategies that companies pursue within an industry which then makes it difficult for an industry to adapt to environmental changes (Miles, Snow and Sharfman 1993). These dynamics are exacerbated when an industry enters the decline stage of the industry life cycle as more companies exit and concentration intensifies (Karniouchina et al. 2013). Thus, as an industry matures, it becomes less capable of adapting to the exogeneous changes that can cause decline.

There is also another key factor that can cause decline over the lifespan of industries. Several studies have shown how the depletion of resources (Haber, Maurer and Razo 2003), the expense of accessing new resources (Slade 2015), or alternative uses of those resources (Johnson 2000) can precipitate industry decline. Haber, Maurer and Razo's (2003) study of the Mexican oil industry draws the poignant conclusion that "Mexico's petroleum industry went into decline because Mexico ran out of oil" (p. 2). Thus, natural resources can limit the lifespan of industries and cause decline. Together, these causes related to industry maturity are often associated with a decline in industry output and size.

Legislation and policy

The fifth category of causes of industry decline concentrates on changes to legislation and public policy. These changes are often portrayed as shocks to the health of industries and the ways in which they operate. Some of these changes directly affect whether products can be sold in foreign markets through trade restrictions (Piper 2010), or their trade can be restricted or phased out in a target market due to the environmental hazard the products may cause (Lieberman 1990). These restrictions limit an industry's sales. For instance, Lieberman's (1990) analysis of the US chemical industry highlighted that decline in ten out of 30 chemical product categories was because the chemical itself was found to be environmentally hazardous or because the chemical was used in a product that was found to be hazardous.

In addition to restricting sales, legislative and policy changes can influence a company's relationships with its business partners (Chatterji and Fabrizio 2016; Griffin, Youm and Vivari 2021). For instance, Chatterji and Fabrizio (2016) show how the Department of Justice investigation of the US orthopedic industry and the ensuing agreement precluded orthopedic companies from collaborating with physicians that reduced that capability of the industry to commercialize innovations that originated from practicing orthopedic physicians. This change slowed the industry's rate of innovation. We can therefore conclude that changes in legislation and public policy can cause almost any form of decline based on how the change affects the industry.

Exogenous events

As the final category of causes for industry decline, we single out exogenous events. These events have little to do with the industries themselves or their competitive potency, and they cannot be predicted. Some of them are 'black swans' that emerge suddenly in the social and business environment of an industry. This category includes events such as the global financial crisis of 2007 (Huhtala et al. 2014; Lai 2010), terrorist attacks such as the September 11, 2001, attack in the United States (Corbo, Corrado and Ferriani 2016; Wang, Aggarwal and Wu 2020), wars (Bakker 2005), and the Covid-19 pandemic that began in 2020 (Hitt, Arregle and Holmes 2021; Rouleau, Hällgren and de Rond 2021).

Events like these can suddenly change how an industry operates and drastically alter its future prospects. This can entail changes to the demand conditions of an industry, sudden incapacity of an industry to renew itself, or reshuffling of roles and relationships within an industry. A selection of examples from the literature can help to outline what these changes mean. Wang, Aggarwal and Wu (2020) demonstrated how the September 11 attacks transformed the technology-related preferences of the US Department of Defense that led US defense industry to hastily adapt to this demand-side shock. Bakker (2005) analyzed how the First World War prevented the European film industry from adapting to new quality requirements set for films since the war prevented them from investing in new technologies that would have enabled them to enter a 'quality race' against Hollywood. Corbo, Corrado and Ferriani (2016) analyzed how September 11 altered the airline industry by changing the structure of the airline field. These examples show that exogenous shocks can create any kind of decline based on its effect on an industry.

What happens during industry decline

Decline causes adjustments on the company and industry levels. It is therefore worthwhile to outline what researchers have discovered about the events and dynamics pertaining to the processes of decline. We provide separate analyses for continuous and discontinuous decline processes. This is based on Zammuto and Cameron's (1982) claim that "continuous change represents relatively predictable change; discontinuous change represents sudden or unexpected change where the past is not a good predictor of the future" (p. 251). This distinction naturally affects the ways in which industries and companies adjust to decline.

Continuous decline processes

Continuous decline is arguably the most widely analyzed form of decline and there are identifiable strands of research that have analyzed its dimensions. Continuous decline is the reduction in industry size that can take place through jobs losses, diminishing industry output, or reduction in the number of companies. The adjustment begins slowly as managers see the need to adjust to the decline (Zammuto and Cameron 1982). These adjustments can happen in several ways. Continuous decline can mean closing down production facilities and decline in overall production (Lai 2010; Lie 2008) or hollowing out the industry as multinational companies relocate their production facilities to lower-cost countries (Donnelly, Begley and Collis 2017; McGovern 2011). It can also entail a wave of business exits and consolidations as the number of actors decreases, while their efficiency increases (Karniouchina et al. 2013; Morrow, Johnson and Busenitz 2004; Ruef 2004). Continuous decline can also be associated with the dissolution of industries when companies become associated with related industries (Kuilman and van Driel 2013) or when they begin to migrate to new and emerging industries (Klepper and Simons 2000). In doing so, while the focal industry slowly ceases to exist, the companies formerly associated with the industry continue to operate in related industries.

In understanding the process of continuous decline, industry life-cycle theory offers a central explanation (see Peltoniemi 2011 for an overview). Depending on the study, industry life cycles have been depicted as consisting of three or four stages, including introduction, growth, and maturity (Klepper 1997) followed by decline (Karniouchina et al. 2013; Miles, Snow and Sharfman 1993). Klepper (1997) depicted the first three stages as follows in his seminal study:

> In the initial, exploratory or embryonic stage, market volume is low, uncertainty is high, the product design is primitive, and unspecialized machinery is used to manufacture the product. Many firms enter and competition based on product innovation is intense. In the second, intermediate or growth stage, output growth is high, the design of the product begins to stabilize, product innovation declines, and the production process becomes more refined as specialized machinery is substituted for labor. Entry slows and a shakeout of producers occurs. Stage three, the mature stage, corresponds to a mature market. Output growth slows, entry declines further, market shares stabilize, innovations are less significant, and management, marketing, and manufacturing techniques become more refined.
>
> (p. 148)

Following these three stages, the last stage of the industry life cycle is decline. This is where demand for industry output begins to decrease (Dinlersoz and MacDonald 2009). In this stage, more firms exit the industry (due to bankruptcies and/or increased mergers and acquisitions) and the industry becomes concentrated around a few companies that compete intensely for the contracting market (Karniouchina et al. 2013). At the same time, variety in competitive strategies continues to decrease (Miles, Snow and Sharfman 1993) as companies focus on increasing efficiency to stay competitive (Karniouchina et al. 2013). Figure 2.2 depicts the industry life cycle in terms of industry output and the number of producers.

On the basis of this depiction of industry life cycles, we can make several crucial remarks. If we look at decline only in terms of the number of

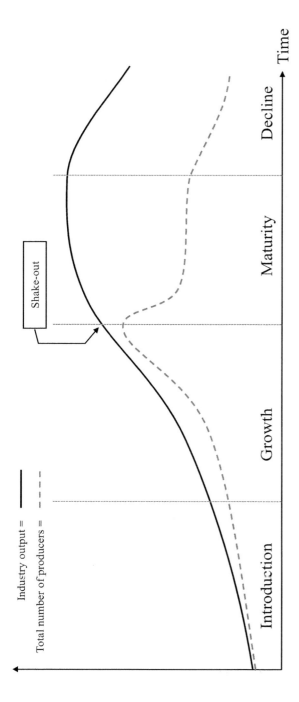

Industry output =

Total number of producers =

Shake-out

Introduction

Growth

Maturity

Decline

Time

Figure 2.2 Illustration of the industry life cycle

companies, then shake-out, during which smaller companies exit, could be understood as a form of decline. However, since industry output still grows after the shake-out, it cannot be said to constitute decline. Only when both industry output and the number of companies begin to diminish can we say that an industry has entered the stage of decline (Dinlersoz and MacDonald 2009). Therefore, if we approach decline from the perspective of industry life cycles, decline happens when both industry output and the number of companies begin to drop.

The interrelated role of shrinking industry output and drop in the number of companies segues into a discussion of how these two factors interact during decline. To understand this, a strand of research has focused on these dynamics, set in motion by the seminal studies of Ghemawat and Nalebuff (1985, 1990). These studies provide key insights into capacity reduction and business exit during decline.

The primary form of business exit changes during the decline process. In the early stages of decline, exit happens through merger and acquisitions. When decline persists over time, business exit starts to happen through voluntary liquidations, while exit during the late stage of decline happens through bankruptcies (Schary 1991). This is partly because large firms can mitigate the need for exit by acquiring their smaller competitors when decline begins (Filson and Songsamphant 2005). However, the companies that exit through mergers and acquisitions still contribute to the industry output, whereas the companies that are dissolved truly exit the industry and decrease the output of the industry (Lamberg and Peltoniemi 2020). In this way, mergers and acquisitions in the early stage of decline contribute to industry concentration, whereas voluntary liquidations and bankruptcies adjust industry output in the later stages.

In their study of decline, Ghemawat and Nalebuff (1990) described the pattern of capacity adjustment in the following way:

> In this equilibrium the largest of several equally efficient firms will reduce capacity alone until its market share is equal to that of its next smallest rival. Once parity is reached, the two largest firms reduce capacity together while all others maintain capacity. Then, when they reach the size of the third biggest firm, all three start to shrink at an equal rate, and so on.
>
> (p. 170)

At a first glance, it seems that large firms bear the brunt of decline while smaller firms are shielded from it. However, this might not always be the case, since Lieberman (1990) found that while large firms are forced to cut capacity, they still outlast their smaller and less efficient rivals.

To make these process dynamics even more complicated, exit usually happens with a delay. This is because companies wait to see whether their competitors will exit before them, which would give them a larger market share (Takahashi 2015). This naturally makes the process of business exits inefficient as companies may sustain losses for long periods while they try to wait out their competitors.

Taken together, these studies demonstrate some of the key dynamics related to capacity adjustment and business exit during decline. Therefore, this strand of research gives us an understanding of how industries respond to the process of decline when the focus is settled purely on how industries (and the constituent companies) adjust their output during decline and how this forces some companies to exit the industry.

Beyond interfirm dynamics related to capacity adjustments and business exits, different interventions from governments and trade associations are not uncommon in order to slow down or direct the decline process. This can mean the introduction of import tariffs to protect the local industry and to slow the decline without affecting how the industry operates (Brainard and Verdier 1997; Cassing and Hillman 1986; Hillman 1982). However, interventions can also be directed toward industry rationalization where less effective production units are closed down (Lazonick 1983), while more competitive ones are subsidized so that they can increase their efficiency (Garside 2005). The influence of interventions therefore depends on whether they are targeted to slow down the decline or restructuring the industry so that it could regain its international competitiveness.

Finally, beyond the doom and gloom of capacity reduction and business exits, decline can lead to a rebound or reemergence. Industries can rebound by focusing on new markets as their share of the current markets melts away. Kalafsky and MacPherson (2002) recount how the US machine tool industry that had been in decline for over 20 years due to increasing imports was recovering because of a newfound focus on exports and niche markets. Industries can also survive or reemerge after the introduction of new dominant technologies that supplant the technology that a declining industry relies upon. This can be done by retreating to a market niche or by finding a new application for the old technology (Adner and Snow 2010). These actions can reverse the decline and secure a smaller market for an industry that operates with outdated technology. There is also the possibility of technology reemergence which has been the case with the Swiss watch industry that has been able to redefine the meanings and values associated with mechanical watches in contrast to the technologically more advanced quartz watches (Raffaelli 2019). This enabled the industry to reverse the protracted decline and achieve market growth again. Industries can also regenerate themselves through structural changes. Fasenfest and Jacobs (2003) analyzed how southern Michigan's auto industry regenerated itself by transitioning away from manufacturing and moved toward technical centers that conduct activities such as design and prototyping. Therefore, while the process of decline can be painful, there is a possibility that an industry can eventually recover.

Discontinuous decline processes

Sudden or unpredictable changes can create discontinuous decline processes. Managers are highly aware of these unusual events (Zammuto and Cameron 1982) but adjusting to them can be challenging. For instance, the Covid-19 pandemic is a good example of discontinuous decline since it and its effects were impossible to foresee. To understand the Covid-19 pandemic and its aftermath, Hitt, Arregle and Holmes (2021) note:

> In the ongoing Covid-19 pandemic, firms must devise strategies to deal with short-term discontinuities and significant uncertainty to survive. After the pandemic eases, longer-term strategic changes may be needed to navigate the competitive landscape arising in the 'New Normal' which has resulted from technological, sociopolitical, and institutional changes (Ahlstrom et al. 2020) that resemble the causes of environmental jolts explained by Meyer et al. (1990).
>
> (p. 1)

This shows how an event of discontinuity and its aftermath can be hard to read. Because discontinuous decline materializes from unpredictable change, it is impossible to paint a comprehensive picture of it. Thus, we will focus on the more common forms of discontinuous decline and how they can influence an industry.

Discontinuous decline can result from singular events that change customer behavior. In some industries, this can mean a plunge in demand which leads to an industry collapse as first output and then employment drop. Lai (2010) analyzed how the 2007 financial crisis led to the collapse of China's export-oriented industries. A sudden drop in demand caused a collapse in industry output and then mass unemployment. However, companies can consolidate capacity within a declining market or redeploy their assets to serve related markets to compensate for declining demand. The ramifications of these choices are what Anand and Singh (1997) analyzed in their seminal study of asset redeployment, acquisitions, and strategy in declining industries. When customer preferences suddenly change, companies can also adapt their capabilities to match these changes that might also transform the industry itself. Wang, Aggarwal and Wu (2020) analyzed how the US defense adapted to changes in defense contracting by using their technological capabilities and customer relationships.

Discontinuous decline can also emerge from the dynamics of industry boom and bust. This can take place either as a singular boom of an industry followed by a bust or as boom and bust cycles (or business cycles) on the level of national economies. A singular boom followed by a bust is often characterized by an opportunity that induces mass entry into and then mass exodus from an industry (Boothman 2000; Filatotchev and Toms 2003). Boothman's (2000) study of the Canadian pulp and paper industry is a telling example. He recounts how during the 1920s Canadian pulp and paper industry grew and ended up producing twice what the market demanded. As a consequence, the industry started struggling in 1928. By 1932, half of the companies in the industry were bankrupt and the other half were insolvent. The reasons for this rapid collapse can be located in overinvestment and overcapacity of the industry that was made possible by dubious corporate reporting practices. In addition to singular events, industries are also susceptible to boom and bust cycles. During these cycles, companies shift their focus from customers and innovation toward competition and efficiency when decline takes place to remain competitive (Dugal and Morbey 1995; Huhtala et al. 2014). Thus, these cycles are characterized by the ebbs and flows of market creation and market defense as the economic situation changes.

Finally, legislative changes are the third form of discontinuous decline. They can force a change in business relations and how economic activities are organized within an industry (Chatterji and Fabrizio 2016; Griffin, Youm and Vivari 2021). For instance, Griffin, Youm and Vivari (2021) explained how American tobacco firms adapted to the Master Settlement Agreement by reorganizing their value chain activities and sociopolitical relations in order to operate within the bounds of social approval. Therefore, the impact and consequent adaptation by companies depend on how legislative changes affect an industry.

How industry decline can be managed

Until this point, we have diagnosed decline, its possible causes, and the kind of processes it can generate. What we have not mentioned is how decline can be managed. To explain how decline can be managed, we provide separate analyses for the industry and company levels (see Figure 2.3). This is because the managerial responses to decline differ depending on whether we are discussing industries (i.e., populations of companies) or individual companies that compete against each other. This also foregrounds the fact that decline can be managed on both the industry and company levels.

Managing decline on the industry level

Managing decline on the industry level is concentrated on the mitigation of two threats: international competition and substitution by other industries. An obvious way to counteract decline is to minimize the possibility of it occurring. One way to do this is by promoting competitive variety within a local industry since decline is often characterized by the lack of variation that makes an industry susceptible to external threats (Miles, Snow and Sharfman 1993).

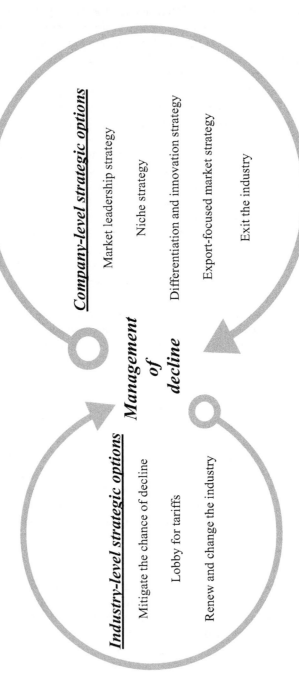

Figure 2.3 Strategic options for managing decline on the industry and company levels

While this may seem negative from the perspective of individual companies, competitive variety can cushion or postpone decline on the industry level. Similarly, sustaining innovation within an industry can deter decline since it enables industries to adapt. Arora, Branstetter and Drev (2013) argued that Silicon Valley was able to overtake Japan in the global IT industry because it was more adaptable when focus moved from hardware to software.

When a local industry enters decline due to international competition, tariff barriers can cushion the blow by limiting imports to the local market. The political influence of industries plays a key role in tariff setting since it affects how industries can affect public authorities' political self-interest to erect tariffs (Hillman 1982). While tariffs tend to persist once they have been erected, they do not address the core issue, which is that companies operate sub-optimally compared to foreign competitors (Brainard and Verdier 1997). Tariffs can therefore become a risky way to manage decline since further erosion of an industry can affect its economic and political importance that make government support possible (Cassing and Hillman 1986). Thus, tariffs can offset decline but they do not address its cause.

Industries often need change and renewal to prevent decline. This can occur through innovation, redefinition of target markets, or transformation of industry structures. When industries enter a state of decline, the rate of innovation tends to decrease (Dugal and Morbey 1995). This is a key issue since innovation generates flexibility and enables adaptation (Freedman and Blair 2010; Hitt, Arregle and Holmes 2021), while providing opportunities for companies to enter new industries (Klepper and Simons 2000). Similarly, redefining target markets can expedite renewal. In practice, this can mean focusing on export and niche markets when competitors start to overtake the domestic market (Adner and Snow 2010; Kalafsky and MacPherson 2002). These changes can also alter the industry structure. For instance, incumbent firms can be replaced by more specialized companies that employ a more highly skilled workforce (Fasenfest and Jacobs 2003). These shifts in focus can offset decline caused by international competition by redefining the industry.

Managing decline on the company level

Companies can manage decline or even become successful during decline in several ways. Many of these strategic alternatives have already been outlined by Harrigan in her seminal studies on strategy formulation in declining industries (Harrigan 1980; Harrigan and Porter 1983). Where this is the case, we will start by charting out their suggestions which are then followed by supportive evidence from other studies.

Harrigan (1980; Harrigan and Porter 1983) suggested market share leadership as a strategic alternative during decline. By increasing efficiency and market power, a company can control the decline process and avoid price competition. Anand and Singh (1997) found support for this idea in the declining US defense industry where consolidation-oriented acquisitions outperform diversification-oriented acquisitions in terms of both stock market performance and operating performance. Similarly, Morrow, Johnson and Busenitz (2004) found that reducing cost is more conducive to firm performance than reduction of assets during decline. The process of becoming a market share leader can also be expedited by acquiring smaller rivals; this mitigates the need to exit the industry as decline starts to take its toll (Filson and Songsamphant 2005). By applying this strategy, a company can ensure that it stays competitive against its rivals as competition intensifies and further companies exit the industry.

Harrigan (1980; Harrigan and Porter 1983) also suggested the alterative of a niche strategy. Her rationale was that a company should focus on market segments that might not decline at all or which decline slower than the mainstream market. In line with this suggestion, Bumgardner et al. (2011) studied the declining US housing construction market and concluded that smaller firms and firms that focus on made-to-order houses were more likely to see increased sales volumes during decline because of their focus on market niches.

Focusing on differentiation and innovation is another avenue to succeed in declining industries. By studying the value propositions of high growth firms in declining industries, Chandler, Broberg and Allison (2014) found:

> In our analysis, it appears that high-growth firms in declining industries create unique value propositions by: (1) focusing on meeting the specific needs of an underserved market segment; (2) identifying a new market segment by focusing on product or service characteristics that appeal to customers who prefer the product innovation to the mainstream product; or (3) providing a total customer solution instead of focusing just on the product.
>
> (p. 249)

Similarly, Bamiatzi and Kirchmaier (2014) revealed that small- and medium-sized companies that grow during decline combine a differentiation strategy through innovation with a product customization. Therefore, the ability to find unserved customer needs and satisfy them with innovative or customized offerings can lead to success during decline.

When industries enter a decline phase due to increased imports, focus on export markets can provide a much-needed remedy. Kalafsky and MacPherson (2002) give a good example of this since their study shows how US manufacturers in the machine tool industry rebounded by focusing on export and niche markets. Further insight into export market expansion is offered by Lie (2008), who shows that when the European fertilizer market went into decline, Norsk Hydro was able to expand into competitors' markets since the repercussions of competitive retaliation were lower than the potential gains of market entry. This was because Norsk Hydro entered substantially larger markets than their Norwegian home market.

Finally, following Harrigan (1980; Harrigan and Porter 1983), a company can exit the declining industry by harvesting its assets or by doing a quick divestment. On the one hand, the logic behind harvesting is to disinvest in a controlled manner and milk as much profit out of the assets as possible. On the other hand, quick divestment rests on the idea that assets can be sold at a profit early in the decline.

We can therefore conclude that there are several strategic alternatives for companies operating in declining industries. Decisions on which of these can be followed depend on company and industry factors. Company size is a crucial determinant since market leadership is a more suitable strategy for incumbents; a niche strategy is more natural choice for smaller companies. Likewise, the possibility to focus on differentiation and innovation or export markets is dictated by market conditions and customer behavior. Thus, to succeed in declining industries, managers have to find strategies that align with the characteristics of their company and the possibilities in the business environment.

Summary

This chapter summarized research on industry decline and how decline can be managed. It focused on four areas: what constitutes decline, what causes decline, what happens during decline, and how decline can be managed.

To answer *what constitutes decline*, we presented three classes of decline and their central indicators. These three classes cover different ways in which an industry can experience decline:

1 Decline in output and industry size (decrease in industry output, the number of companies, or loss in jobs)
2 Market decline (decline in sales, demand, or market share)
3 Decline in industry renewal (decline in innovation or investments)

To understand how industries can end up in a state of decline, we have examined *what causes industry decline*. This led us to pinpoint six causes for industry decline:

1 Customer behavior (decrease in customer spending or change in needs)
2 Innovation (especially lack of innovation)
3 Market dynamics (international competition or fall in the price of an industry's output)

4 Industry maturity (maturity that precludes adaptation or leads to depletion of resources)
5 Legislation and policy (restricting the sales of goods or influencing relationships)
6 Exogenous events (singular events that change established dimensions of an industry)

We then examined *what happens during industry decline* by analyzing continuous and discontinuous decline processes. With regard to the former, we have foregrounded industry life cycles and the dynamics of capacity adjustment and business exits as explanations of what happens during decline. In addition, we discussed the role of government interventions during decline and the possibility of industry renewal and rebound. In terms of the latter, we analyzed how companies respond to singular events that change customer behavior, how they respond to industry booms and busts, and how companies adapt to legislative changes. Each of these discontinuities generated a different response.

Finally, we outlined *how decline can be managed* on the industry and company levels. On the industry level, we highlighted that decline can be mitigated through competition and innovation, by lobbying for tariff barriers when decline takes place, or through industry renewal and change that can help redefine an industry and offset the decline. On the company level, we outlined five strategies:

1 Adopt a market leadership strategy (focus on efficiency and market power)
2 Adopt a niche strategy (focus on market segments that decline more slowly than the mainstream market)
3 Focus on differentiation and innovation (find unmet market needs that can be satisfied through innovation or product customization)
4 Focus on export markets to mitigate losses in home market (offset losses in home market by exporting)
5 Exit the industry by either harvesting assets or doing a quick divestment (milk assets or sell them when decline begins)

These analyses enable the reader to identify reasons for industry, analyze what the decline process will likely mean, and what strategic options there are for adapting to decline. These takeaways are summarized in Figure 2.4.

Suggestions for further reading

In order to get further acquainted with industry decline, there are a number of studies that we suggest for further reading. First, to get a complementary view of what causes industry decline, the recent study by Lamberg, Ojala

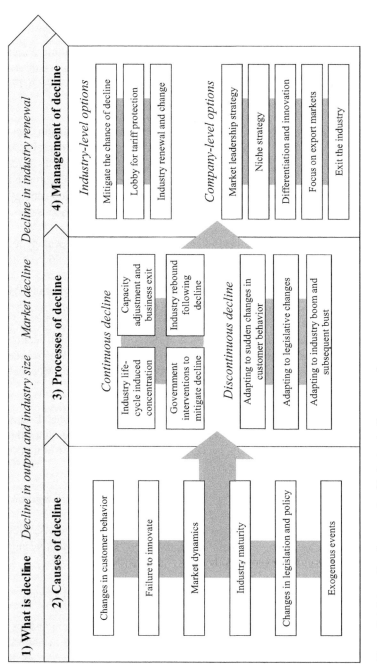

Figure 2.4 Integrative framework of industry decline research

and Peltoniemi (2018) provides a good overview of research by focusing on historical and longitudinal studies.

- Lamberg, J. A., Ojala, J., & Peltoniemi, M. (2018). Thinking about industry decline: A qualitative meta-analysis and future research directions. *Business History*, *60*(2), 127–156. DOI: 10.1080/00076791.2017. 1340943

In this chapter, we referred to studies that draw from the population ecology of organizations. The seminal study by Hannan and Freeman (1977) outlines the key tenets of the perspective. We also suggest an article by Ruef (2004) that tests the key mechanisms that explain processes of decline and resurgence. Finally, Zammuto and Cameron (1982) use population ecology to outline different forms of decline and potential managerial responses.

- Hannan, M. T., & Freeman, J. (1977). The population ecology of organizations. *American Journal of Sociology*, *82*(5), 929–964. DOI: 10.1086/226424
- Ruef, M. (2004). For whom the bell tolls: Ecological perspectives on industrial decline and resurgence. *Industrial and Corporate Change*, *13*(1), 61–89. DOI: 10.1093/icc/13.1.61
- Zammuto, R. F., & Cameron, K. S. (1982). Environmental decline and organizational response. In *Academy of Management Proceedings 1982*(1), (pp. 250–254). Briarcliff Manor, NY: Academy of Management. DOI: 10.5465/ambpp.1982.4976626

Another perspective covered in this chapter is industry life cycles. In this regard, we suggest reading Klepper's seminal 1997 study that outlines the key ideas regarding industry life cycles as well as the 2011 review of industry life-cycle research by Peltoniemi.

- Klepper, S. (1997). Industry life cycles. *Industrial and Corporate Change*, *6*(1), 145–182. DOI: 10.1093/icc/6.1.145
- Peltoniemi, M. (2011). Reviewing industry life-cycle theory: Avenues for future research. *International Journal of Management Reviews*, *13*(4), 349–375. DOI: 10.1111/j.1468–2370.2010.00295.x

To understand management during decline, we suggest Harrigan's work.

- Harrigan, K. R. (1980). Strategy formulation in declining industries. *Academy of Management Review*, 5(4), 599–604. DOI: 10.5465/ amr.1980.4288965

• Harrigan, K. R., & Porter, M. E. (1983). End-game strategies for declining industries. *Harvard Business Review*, 61(4), 111–120.

Note

1 Lamberg, Ojala and Peltoniemi (2018) identified that decline can be caused by 1) policy and institutional environment, 2) market dynamics, 3) technology, and 4) capabilities.

References

Adner, R., & Snow, D. (2010). Old technology responses to new technology threats: Demand heterogeneity and technology retreats. *Industrial and Corporate Change*, 19(5), 1655–1675. https://doi.org/10.1093/icc/dtq046

Amankwah-Amoah, J. (2015). Explaining declining industries in developing countries: The case of textiles and apparel in Ghana. *Competition & Change*, 19(1), 19–35. https://doi.org/10.1177/1024529414563004

Anand, J., & Singh, H. (1997). Asset redeployment, acquisitions and corporate strategy in declining industries. *Strategic Management Journal*, 18(S1), 99–118.

Arora, A., Branstetter, L. G., & Drev, M. (2013). Going soft: How the rise of software-based innovation led to the decline of Japan's IT industry and the resurgence of Silicon Valley. *Review of Economics and Statistics*, 95(3), 757–775. https://doi.org/10.1162/REST_a_00286

Bakker, G. (2005). The decline and fall of the European film industry: Sunk costs, market size, and market structure, 1890–1927. *The Economic History Review*, 58(2), 310–351. https://doi.org/10.1111/j.1468-0289.2005.00306.x

Bamiatzi, V. C., & Kirchmaier, T. (2014). Strategies for superior performance under adverse conditions: A focus on small and medium-sized high-growth firms. *International Small Business Journal*, 32(3), 259–284. https://doi.org/10.1177/0266242612459534

Baptista, R., & Karaöz, M. (2011). Turbulence in growing and declining industries. *Small Business Economics*, 36(3), 249–270. https://doi.org/10.1007/s11187-009-9226-2

Boothman, B. E. (2000). High finance/low strategy: Corporate collapse in the Canadian pulp and paper industry, 1919–1932. *Business History Review*, 74(4), 611–656. https://doi.org/10.2307/3116469

Brainard, S. L., & Verdier, T. (1997). The political economy of declining industries: Senescent industry collapse revisited. *Journal of International Economics*, 42(1–2), 221–237. https://doi.org/10.1016/S0022-1996(96)01432-8

Bumgardner, M., Buehlmann, U., Schuler, A., & Crissey, J. (2011). Competitive actions of small firms in a declining market. *Journal of Small Business Management*, 49(4), 578–598. https://doi.org/10.1111/j.1540-627X.2011.00337.x

Cassing, J. H., & Hillman, A. L. (1986). Shifting comparative advantage and senescent industry collapse. *The American Economic Review*, 76(3), 516–523.

Chandler, G. N., Broberg, J. C., & Allison, T. H. (2014). Customer value propositions in declining industries: Differences between industry representative and high-growth firms. *Strategic Entrepreneurship Journal, 8*(3), 234–253. https://doi.org/10.1002/sej.1181

Chatterji, A. K., & Fabrizio, K. R. (2016). Does the market for ideas influence the rate and direction of innovative activity? Evidence from the medical device industry. *Strategic Management Journal, 37*(3), 447–465. https://doi.org/10.1002/smj.2340

Corbo, L., Corrado, R., & Ferriani, S. (2016). A new order of things: Network mechanisms of field evolution in the aftermath of an exogenous shock. *Organization Studies, 37*(3), 323–348. https://doi.org/10.1177/0170840615613373

Dinlersoz, E. M., & MacDonald, G. (2009). The industry life-cycle of the size distribution of firms. *Review of Economic Dynamics, 12*(4), 648–667. https://doi.org/10.1016/j.red.2009.01.001

Donnelly, T., Begley, J., & Collis, C. (2017). The West Midlands automotive industry: The road downhill. *Business History, 59*(1), 56–74. https://doi.org/10.1080/00076791.2016.1235559

Dugal, S. S., & Morbey, G. K. (1995). Revisiting corporate R&D spending during a recession. *Research-Technology Management, 38*(4), 23–27. https://doi.org/10.1080/08956308.1995.11674276

Fasenfest, D., & Jacobs, J. (2003). An anatomy of change and transition: The automobile industry of Southeast Michigan. *Small Business Economics, 21*(2), 153–172. https://doi.org/10.1023/A:1025018626406

Filatotchev, I., & Toms, S. (2003). Corporate governance, strategy and survival in a declining industry: A study of UK cotton textile companies. *Journal of Management Studies, 40*(4), 895–920. https://doi.org/10.1111/1467-6486.00364

Filson, D., & Songsamphant, B. (2005). Horizontal mergers and exit in declining industries. *Applied Economics Letters, 12*(2), 129–132. https://doi.org/10.1080/13504850042000314334

Freedman, C., & Blair, A. (2010). Seeds of destruction: The decline and fall of the US car industry. *The Economic and Labour Relations Review, 21*(1), 105–126. https://doi.org/10.1177/103530461002100109

Garside, W. R. (2005). A very British phenomenon? Industrial politics and the decline of the Japanese coal mining industry since the 1950s. *Australian Economic History Review, 45*(2), 186–203. https://doi.org/10.1111/j.1467-8446.2005.00134.x

Ghemawat, P., & Nalebuff, B. (1985). Exit. *The RAND Journal of Economics, 16*(2), 184–194.

Ghemawat, P., & Nalebuff, B. (1990). The devolution of declining industries. *The Quarterly Journal of Economics, 105*(1), 167–186. https://doi.org/10.2307/2937824

Griffin, J. J., Youm, Y. N., & Vivari, B. (2021). Stakeholder engagement strategies after an exogenous shock: How Philip Morris and RJ Reynolds adapted differently to the 1998 master settlement agreement. *Business & Society, 60*(4), 1009–1036. https://doi.org/10.1177/0007650319870818

Haber, S., Maurer, N., & Razo, A. (2003). When the law does not matter: The rise and decline of the Mexican oil industry. *The Journal of Economic History, 63*(1), 1–32. https://doi.org/10.1017/S0022050703001712

Hannan, M. T., & Freeman, J. (1977). The population ecology of organizations. *American Journal of Sociology, 82*(5), 929–964. https://doi.org/10.1086/226424

Harrigan, K. R. (1980). Strategy formulation in declining industries. *Academy of Management Review, 5*(4), 599–604. https://doi.org/10.5465/amr.1980.4288965

Harrigan, K. R., & Porter, M. E. (1983). End-game strategies for declining industries. *Harvard Business Review, 61*(4), 111–120.

Higgins, D., & Toms, S. (2003). Financial distress, corporate borrowing, and industrial decline: The Lancashire cotton spinning industry, 1918–38. *Accounting, Business & Financial History, 13*(2), 207–232. https://doi.org/10.1080/0958520032000084996

Hillman, A. L. (1982). Declining industries and political-support protectionist motives. *The American Economic Review, 72*(5), 1180–1187.

Hitt, M. A., Arregle, J. L., & Holmes Jr, R. M. (2021). Strategic management theory in a post-pandemic and non-ergodic world. *Journal of Management Studies, 58*(1), 259–264. https://doi.org/10.1111/joms.12646

Huhtala, J. P., Sihvonen, A., Frösén, J., Jaakkola, M., & Tikkanen, H. (2014). Market orientation, innovation capability and business performance: Insights from the global financial crisis. *Baltic Journal of Management, 9*(2), 134–152. https://doi.org/10.1108/BJM-03-2013-0044

Johnson, R. N. (2000). Declining industries and the persistence of government support programs: The quiet decline of gum naval stores production in the United States. *The Journal of Economic History, 60*(4), 995–1016. https://doi.org/10.1017/S0022050700026346

Kalafsky, R. V., & MacPherson, A. D. (2002). The competitive characteristics of US manufacturers in the machine tool industry. *Small Business Economics, 19*(4), 355–369. https://doi.org/10.1023/A:1019676202588

Karniouchina, E. V., Carson, S. J., Short, J. C., & Ketchen Jr, D. J. (2013). Extending the firm vs. industry debate: Does industry life cycle stage matter? *Strategic Management Journal, 34*(8), 1010–1018. https://doi.org/10.1002/smj.2042

Klepper, S. (1997). Industry life cycles. *Industrial and Corporate Change, 6*(1), 145–182. https://doi.org/10.1093/icc/6.1.145

Klepper, S., & Simons, K. L. (2000). Dominance by birthright: Entry of prior radio producers and competitive ramifications in the US television receiver industry. *Strategic Management Journal, 21*(10–11), 997–1016.

Kuilman, J. G., & van Driel, H. (2013). You too, Brutus? Category demise in Rotterdam warehousing, 1871–2011. *Industrial and Corporate Change, 22*(2), 511–548. https://doi.org/10.1093/icc/dts019

Lai, P. (2010). External demand decline-caused industry collapse in China. *China & World Economy, 18*(1), 47–62. https://doi.org/10.1111/j.1749-124X.2010.01180.x

Lamberg, J. A., Ojala, J., & Peltoniemi, M. (2018). Thinking about industry decline: A qualitative meta-analysis and future research directions. *Business History, 60*(2), 127–156. https://doi.org/10.1080/00076791.2017.1340943

Lamberg, J. A., & Peltoniemi, M. (2020). The nanoeconomics of firm-level decision-making and industry evolution: Evidence from 200 years of paper and pulp making. *Strategic Management Journal, 41*(3), 499–529. https://doi.org/10.1002/smj.3080

Lazonick, W. (1981). Competition, specialization, and industrial decline. *Journal of Economic History, 41*(1), 31–38. https://doi.org/10.1017/S0022050700042716

Lazonick, W. (1983). Industrial organization and technological change: The decline of the British cotton industry. *Business History Review*, *57*(2), 195–236. https://doi.org/10.2307/3114355

Lie, E. (2008). Market power and market failure: The decline of the European Fertilizer Industry and the Expansion of Norsk Hydro. *Enterprise & Society*, *9*(1), 70–95. https://doi.org/10.1093/es/khm084

Lieberman, M. B. (1990). Exit from declining industries: "shakeout" or "stakeout"? *The RAND Journal of Economics*, 538–554.

McCloskey, D. N. (1973). *Economic Maturity and Entrepreneurial Decline: British Iron and Steel, 1870–1913*. Cambridge, MA: Harvard University Press.

McGovern, T. (2011). The decline of the British tyre industry: An evaluation of the policies of the Tyre Industry Sector Working Party. *Business History*, *53*(4), 600–616. https://doi.org/10.1080/00076791.2011.578128

Miles, G., Snow, C. C., & Sharfman, M. P. (1993). Industry variety and performance. *Strategic Management Journal*, *14*(3), 163–177. https://doi.org/10.1002/smj.4250140302

Morrow Jr, J. L., Johnson, R. A., & Busenitz, L. W. (2004). The effects of cost and asset retrenchment on firm performance: The overlooked role of a firm's competitive environment. *Journal of Management*, *30*(2), 189–208. https://doi.org/10.1016/j.jm.2003.01.002

Peltoniemi, M. (2011). Reviewing industry life-cycle theory: Avenues for future research. *International Journal of Management Reviews*, *13*(4), 349–375. https://doi.org/10.1111/j.1468-2370.2010.00295.x

Piper, L. (2010). Parasites from "Alien Shores": The decline of Canada's freshwater fishing industry. *Canadian Historical Review*, *91*(1), 87–114. https://doi.org/10.3138/chr.91.1.87

Porac, J. F., Thomas, H., & Baden-Fuller, C. (2011). Competitive groups as cognitive communities: The case of Scottish knitwear manufacturers revisited. *Journal of Management Studies*, *48*(3), 646–664. https://doi.org/10.1111/j.1467-6486.2010.00988.x

Raffaelli, R. (2019). Technology reemergence: Creating new value for old technologies in Swiss mechanical watchmaking, 1970–2008. *Administrative Science Quarterly*, *64*(3), 576–618. https://doi.org/10.1177/0001839218778505

Rouleau, L., Hällgren, M., & de Rond, M. (2021). Covid-19 and our understanding of risk, emergencies, and crises. *Journal of Management Studies*, *58*(1), 245–248. https://doi.org/10.1111/joms.12649

Ruef, M. (2004). For whom the bell tolls: Ecological perspectives on industrial decline and resurgence. *Industrial and Corporate Change*, *13*(1), 61–89. https://doi.org/10.1093/icc/13.1.61

Schary, M. A. (1991). The probability of exit. *The RAND Journal of Economics*, 339–353.

Sheth, J. N., & Sisodia, R. S. (1999). Revisiting marketing's lawlike generalizations. *Journal of the Academy of Marketing Science*, *27*(1), 71–87. https://doi.org/10.1177/0092070399271006

Slade, M. E. (2015). The rise and fall of an industry: Entry in US copper mining, 1835–1986. *Resource and Energy Economics*, *42*, 141–169. https://doi.org/10.1016/j.reseneeco.2015.08.001

Takahashi, Y. (2015). Estimating a war of attrition: The case of the US movie theater industry. *American Economic Review, 105*(7), 2204–2241. https://doi.org/10.1257/aer.20110701

Wang, T., Aggarwal, V. A., & Wu, B. (2020). Capability interactions and adaptation to demand-side change. *Strategic Management Journal, 41*(9), 1595–1627. https://doi.org/10.1002/smj.3137

Zammuto, R. F., & Cameron, K. S. (1982). Environmental decline and organizational response. *Academy of Management Proceedings, 1982*(1), 250–254. Briarcliff Manor, NY 10510: Academy of Management. https://doi.org/10.5465/ambpp.1982.4976626

3 Cluster and business ecosystem decline

What constitutes cluster decline

Porter's (1990) seminal *The Competitive Advantage of Nations* defined industrial clusters as "a geographically proximate group of interconnected companies and associated institutions in a particular field, linked by commonalities and complementarities" (p. 199; see also Porter 2003). Porter identified clusters as a major source of innovation for industrial policy and the management of economic development (see Saxenian 1983 as an example of similar ideas). Porter's ideas and suggestions revitalized and reformulated some earlier theories on industrial districts (e.g., Becattini 2017; Brusco 1982; Harrison 1992; Pyke, Becattini and Sengenberger 1990) combined with his own normative models of firm strategy (Martin and Sunley 2003). As Trippl et al. (2015) summarizes,

> [w]hile the term "cluster" was introduced by Michael Porter in the 1990s . . . the origins of the notion can be traced back to Marshall's (1920) influential work on industrial districts.
>
> (p. 2028)

Despite its influence, Porter's normative model did not result in enhanced conceptual clarity as Martin and Sunley (2003; see also Martin 1999) aptly note. Researchers still use synonyms like "agglomerations, geographic(al) concentrations, spatial concentrations, localised industries/firms, growth poles, innovative milieu and industrial districts" (Vorley 2008, p. 791). The most recent form of cluster-like research, especially in strategy and innovation studies, operates under the umbrella concept of a business ecosystem (Knight et al. 2020). Although the ecosystem literature originates from other research traditions than the cluster studies (e.g., from complexity theories and system thinking; Peltoniemi 2006), we treat business ecosystems as one more synonym for cluster studies. This choice is warranted as the

DOI: 10.4324/9781003035947-3

definitions of these concepts overlap as can be seen from the following definitions:

> Business ecosystem: "the community of organizations, institutions, and individuals that impact the enterprise and the enterprise's customers and supplies. The relevant community therefore includes complementors, suppliers, regulatory authorities, standard-setting bodies, the judiciary, and educational and research institutions."
>
> (Teece 2007, p. 1325)

> Cluster: "Clusters are constituted by interconnected companies and associated institutions linked by commonalities and complementaries. The links are both vertical (buying and selling chains), and horizontal (complementary products and services, the use of similar specialized inputs, technologies or institutions, and other linkages). Moreover, most of these linkages . . . involve social relationships or networks that produce benefits for the firms involved. The second fundamental characteristic, therefore, is that clusters are geographically proximate groups of interlinked companies."
>
> (Martin and Sunley 2003, p. 10)[1]

Accordingly, the emphasis on both research streams and in our review is on geographically specific groups of firms and other supporting organizations with complementary assets and skills (cf. Bresnahan and Gambardella 2004; Bresnahan, Gambardella and Saxenian 2001; Gordon and McCann 2000; Markusen 1996b). Concomitant to clusters and ecosystems, platforms such as Amazon and Google can be defined as ecosystems that are not geographically oriented but are structured around a stable core that mediates the relationship between a range of complements and end customers (Rietveld, Schilling and Bellavitis 2019).[2] However, for reasons of clarity, we will use the terms *cluster* and *ecosystem* to refer to the different permutations of the same core idea.

The first wave of cluster and ecosystem research, after Porter popularized the approach, offered normative tools to create clusters or ecosystems and identified cases in which researchers had found such success factors. After the initial enthusiasm of the 1990s, the study of the *evolution* of clusters and ecosystems has become important (see Boschma and Fornahl 2011; Cantner et al. 2021; De Propris and Lazzeretti 2009; Menzel and Fornahl 2010; Popp and Wilson 2007; Trippl et al. 2015). These studies focus on the variation, selection, and retention of new technologies, knowledge, and organizations across lifespans of clusters (see Brenner 2004; Menzel and Fornahl 2010; and Popp and Wilson 2007, for a depiction of different stages of cluster life cycle and their key dynamics). For this chapter, it is crucial that the evolutionary research stream also ended up studying the *decline* and potential collapse of local, regional, and national clusters.[3] Following this, we adopt Menzel and Fornahl's (2010, p. 227; see also Belussi and Hervas-Oliver 2016; Hassink 2010a; Hassink 2016) definition of cluster decline:

> A declining cluster is defined by a decrease in the number of companies and especially of employees due to the failures, mergers, and rationalizations. . . . A declining cluster has therefore lost the ability to sustain its diversity, its ability to adjust to changing conditions as well as its potential for an independent renewal.

A cluster therefore runs into difficulties in the creation and maintenance of variation and retention mechanisms and keeping selection mechanisms aligned with market dynamics. The theme of this chapter is to understand how literature has identified factors and processes preventing variation and ways of co-evolving with changing business landscapes.

Throughout the review, we also consider the joint effect of cluster genesis (Simsek, Fox and Heavey 2015) with the presented mechanisms. We divide clusters into two categories: (1) those created by emergence and as a response to market demand (e.g., Bresnahan, Gambardella and Saxenian 2001) and (b) those created by political decisions and planning (Su and Hung 2009; Swords 2013). We do not argue that these two categories would comprehensively fit real-life clusters in which we probably see symbiosis of market-base emergence and policy making. However, for us the two categories refer to the *weighting* of different options from totalitarian planned economies to almost freely emerging market economies.

What causes cluster decline

Our analysis of empirical studies on cluster decline reveals three explanatory categories: factor endowments, knowledge and capabilities, and interorganizational dynamics (see Figure 3.1).[4] These categories are overlapping and potentially contrasting. We do not, however, aim for an exact taxonomy of cluster decline factors but rather look for a more comprehensive explanation and subsequent managerial responses for and to cluster and business ecosystem decline. In the following, we identify these causes and the different factors that fit under each category.

Factor endowments

The first category of reasons to cluster decline concern factor endowments: non-movable (such as land) or semi-permanent resources upon which a cluster's success (and often demise) can be built. In the following we focus

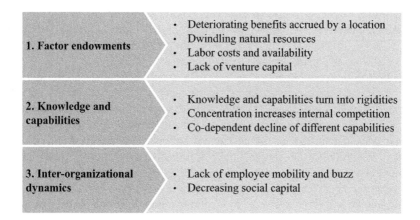

Figure 3.1 Causes of cluster decline

on location, natural resources, labor, and finance as the key decline-related factors that the cluster and ecosystem literatures recognize as important endowment-related factors in cluster decline.

Location

The fundamental explanation of both the genesis and the decline of clusters is geographic location. As Porter (2000) writes,

> Yet the sophistication of how companies compete in a location is strongly influenced by the quality of the microeconomic business environment. Some aspects of the business environment (e.g., the road system, corporate tax rates, the legal system) cut across all industries. These economy-wide (or "horizontal") areas are important and often represent the binding constraints to competitiveness in developing economies. In more advanced economies and increasingly elsewhere, however, the more decisive aspects of the business environment for competitiveness often are cluster specific (e.g., the presence of particular types of suppliers, skills, or university departments).
>
> (p. 19)

The importance of location originates in geography and historical traditions. For example, urban areas such as London have been of economic importance for thousands of years because of their location and population density. Most recently, mega-cities have been seen as naturally suited for the emergence of clusters (Kourtit and Nijkamp 2013). Our analysis identifies vulnerable cities (Naldi, Larsson and Westlund 2020), locations facing dramatic demographic downturn (Kabisch, Haase and Haase 2012), and mono-structure (i.e., dependence on few companies and/or businesses; Blim 1990) as potential factors explaining cluster decline.

Vulnerability and/or rural location of a cluster oftentimes originate in non-market-based genesis of clusters. Nykänen (2018) demonstrates how many contemporary Russian industrial clusters are products of the Soviet Union's economic planning. Likewise, vulnerable cities in Naldi, Larsson and Westlund (2020) are not adjacent to any metropolitan areas and may have been products of economic policies trying to create clusters to support local economies. There is also an interesting logical connection between Porter giving advice on how to create successful clusters, politicians investing money and other resources to locations – not always naturally able to attract economic and innovative activity – and the decline of these artificially created clusters (Martin and Sunley 2003). Swords (2013) demonstrates how Porter's fashionable ideas resulted in policy changes and the creation of clusters in the UK, which did not succeed despite the plans and public investments. Overall, the probability that location becomes a problem is much higher in planning-based clusters than in historically evolved clusters with some natural location-based advantages.

Natural resources

Another obvious reason for cluster decline pertains to natural resources. Some clusters that are "highly dependent upon natural resource inputs are also going to tend to be geographically concentrated – presumably close to the source of those inputs" (Audretsch and Feldman 1996, p. 265). Accordingly, if some products face decreasing demand (Järvinen, Lamberg and Pietinalho 2012) or the natural resources drain (Atta-Mills, Alder and Rashid Sumaila 2004), the cluster may also face decline.

Metal industry clusters (e.g., Treado 2010) tend to be dependent on natural resources. Clusters in commercial agriculture and fishing also share this dependence. Fisheries are especially interesting as decreasing populations of fish species inevitably result in decline of clusters (Baum 1999). When the main source of revenues drains, fishery clusters either marginalize or need to find new sources of revenue (Piper 2010). Similarly, the stigmatization of previously legitimate industries such as whale hunting (Einarsson 2009) may result in cluster decline. Finally, if a key raw material is depleted, the inevitable result is a cluster collapse. Haber, Maurer and Razo's (2003, p. 2) study of the collapse of Mexican oil industry cluster is a vivid example of such dynamics as they show that the reasons for collapse did not originate in institutional changes or market dynamics yet simply on "that Mexico's petroleum industry went into decline because Mexico ran out of oil."

The causal effect of natural resources on cluster decline often conjoins with technological change. We find evidence from the literature in which a new superior technology allows the adaption of new more cost-efficient raw materials resulting in the decline and demise of previously competitive clusters. Paper industry is a case in point concerning especially the adoption of sulfate technology in cellulose production in the 1950s and the 1960s. Compared to sulfite technology, the dominant way of making cellulose before the 1950s, sulfate cellulose is more environmentally friendly, makes possible the making on whiter and glossier printing papers yet it also allowed the use of pine and other previously neglected wood materials – spruce being the most suitable wood material for sulfite cellulose. Accordingly, when companies invested in sulfate cellulose technology, they abandoned earlier factories in spruce-rich areas. In the United States, this meant a cluster decline in the north (Toivanen 2004) when companies moved to the southern states and in Norway an almost total collapse of the entire cluster (Moen 1998). Overall, especially clusters having characteristics of a monoculture – relying on a narrow raw material-base and asset-specific technology system – appear to be highly vulnerable and potential decline cases when environmental parameters change.

Labor

Labor has two effects on cluster decline. Globalization has accelerated competition between economic regions and especially in labor-intensive industries the cost of labor is an important factor in the location of production. Christopherson (2013), for example, shows how the Hollywood film and television production cluster has adapted to the globalization of the industry, with an emphasis on mid-level production budgets. Gertler (1996) shows how a German metal production cluster faced greater challenges from high labor costs and inflexible relationships with trade unions. Potter and Watts' (2010) replication study of Marshall's agglomeration theory and case study gives rather similar results showing that a local pool of skilled labor is an asset for companies hiring them yet at the same time labor costs and total costs tend to increase. This effect also correlates with other cluster effects (local supplier linkages and local knowledge spillovers) resulting in diminishing sales growth and lower profits. Finally, Gittell and Sohl (2005) link increasing wages to decline of clusters.

The second impact related to labor concerns the supply of skilled employees. That skilled labor is important is obvious from basic economic models of industrial organization. Hausmann and Neffke (2019), for example, show

how the rise of industrial production in post-reunification eastern Germany required labor transfer from west to east, underlining the centrality of labor in cluster competitiveness. In the decline phase, Parsons and Rose (2005) show how the skilled labor eventually becomes a liability. The effect comes from overspecialization and is often related to labor costs. In addition, the job market and its functional characteristics are important for the mainte-nance of competitiveness and likewise for decline (Begg 1999). Overall, accompanied with globalization and technological change, different dimen-sions of labor and job markets often join with cluster decline.

Venture capital

The literature links venture capital to cluster decline in three ways: venture capital as a way to slow downward spiraling, lack of venture capital as a cause of decline, and excessive venture capital as a cause of non-natural evolution. Venture capital is an important mechanism in the creation of new variation in economies. This also concerns clusters. A common way of thinking suggests injecting capital into declining clusters (Livi and Jean-nerat 2015; Sun et al. 2019), thus catapulting them onto a renewal path. In contrast, the lack of capital should prevent renewal or even cause cluster decline.

The third problem related to venture capital is intriguing. Whereas the lack of capital is typically seen as a problem of declining clusters linked to mature industries, the detrimental effects of too much capital is a more typi-cal with emerging clusters. Gittell and Sohl (2005), for example, argue that excess venture capital may hinder the emergence of sound business models. Capital may also flow into a narrow set of businesses instead of creating variation into the cluster. Mattsson's (2008) study of the Finnish biotech cluster and similar studies from other countries (Auerswald and Dani 2017; Su and Hung 2009) demonstrate that especially with policy-driven biotech clusters, easily available venture capital has been a life-threatening risk. When the original enthusiasm dissolves, a cluster may easily decline if it lacks naturally generated ties and capabilities. Overall, our material shows that in venture capital as a factor in cluster decline (or renewal) quantity is less important than the quality of venture capital organizations' decision-making processes, importantly including commitment and patience.

Knowledge and capabilities

Another key reason for cluster decline relates to the knowledge and capa-bilities that reside within a cluster, especially when the benefits of concen-tration and specialization of knowledge and capabilities become rigidities (e.g., Bathelt, Malmberg and Maskell 2004; Suire and Vicente 2009). This can lead companies within a cluster to delay innovation and renewal, putting them at a disadvantage against competitors when technology changes rapidly. For instance, Mudambi and colleagues (2017) note that the Akron tire cluster in Ohio was slow to innovate after the introduction of radial tires; this delay contributed to the decline of the cluster. In addition, concentration can increase competition and decrease cooperation within a cluster (Mossig and Schieber 2016). This can have a negative influence on the development and sharing of new knowledge that is a usual benefit of clustering. These ideas are also in line with the capability literature in strategic management which has highlighted that specialized capabilities can turn into rigidities (Leonard-Barton 1992) and that capabilities need to be changed by sensing and seizing opportunities, and by continuously transforming capabilities to take advantage of opportunities (Teece 2007). For cluster and ecosystems, the important question is: who should "sense and seize" these opportunities and manage transformations?

One key dynamic in this area relates to how different capabilities and types of knowledge influence each other when they cause decline – in essence whether their decline is co-dependent. On the one hand, Tomlinson and Branston (2014) described how the long decline of the North Staffordshire ceramics cluster led to the decline of manufacturing within the cluster and to the decline in the technological capabilities related to the development of new ceramic equipment within the district that never bounced back when production started to rebound. On the other hand, in the Detroit auto cluster (Hannigan, Cano-Kollmann and Mudambi 2015) and Akron tire cluster in Ohio (Mudambi et al. 2017), the decline in manufacturing did not disrupt the creation of knowledge within the cluster but rather transformed the cluster to focus on R&D over time.

Interorganizational dynamics

At the elementary level, cluster firms and other organizations are both adjacently located and interconnected. We focus on two most important forms of interconnectedness: employee mobility and social capital.

Employee mobility

In addition to the availability of labor, the lack of employee mobility and general buzz have been pinpointed as contributing factors to cluster decline. While these factors have been claimed as key success factors for the emergence of clusters such as the Silicon Valley (Klepper 2016), numerous studies have argued that the converse is true for declining ecosystems (Brunello and Langella 2016; Cantner et al. 2021; Mossig 2011; Mossig and Schieber 2016). This is in line with Menzel and Fornahl's (2010) theorizing that declining clusters are characterized by concentration and the lack of capability to generate diversity.

These ideas can be elaborated with the help of three examples. First, in theorizing the life cycle of entrepreneurial ecosystems, Cantner and colleagues (2021) conjecture that the decline phase of an entrepreneurial ecosystem is characterized by the exploitation of ideas in existing firms rather than the creation of new firms and ideas. This means that during decline, an entrepreneurial ecosystem with a more emergent and easily adaptive organizational form transforms to a more routinized business ecosystem. Second, by studying data from the Italian labor force, Brunello and Langella (2016) found out that the impact of recession on entrepreneurship was stronger in industrial districts because they thrive on intense social interactions that amplify the negative influence of recessions. Therefore, waning interaction due to economic decline can be a nightmare for a cluster. Third, while labor mobility can disperse localized learning among companies, it can be met with suspicion when the cluster ceases to produce enough variation to sustain diversity among companies (Mossig and Schieber 2016). Overall, we observe that the lack of employee mobility and buzz can cause or contribute to the decline of a cluster by limiting its capacity for renewal.

Social capital

Social capital within clusters can be understood as social networks that enable their members to build trust among each other, develop partnerships, engage in collective action, and access resources such as knowledge (e.g., Naldi, Larsson and Westlund 2020; Su and Hung 2009). This kind of networking and cooperation has been suggested as a success factor for locations such as the Baden-Württemberg region and its machinery industry where small- and medium-sized companies frequently collaborate with each other (Gertler 1996). Diminishing this kind of capital can hinder cooperation and collective action within a cluster that impedes growth and has a negative influence on the health of the cluster (Tomlinson and Branston 2014). As an example of how this can cause decline, Amdam and Bjarnar (2015) analyzed how the Norwegian furniture cluster was able to survive until the 1980s through collective action and collaboration but increasing global competition in the 1990s led some of the companies to offshore their production which negatively influenced cooperation and future prospects of the cluster. Yet, several studies have also shown how networks built especially on innovation can be resilient in the face of decline (Desmarchelier and Zhang 2018) and can crystallize a new function and direction for a cluster that eventually revitalizes it (Hannigan, Cano-Kollmann and Mudambi 2015).

What happens during cluster decline

In the preceding sections, we focused on measurable variables (e.g., changes in labor price, an increase or a decrease of natural resources) that the literature has found to affect cluster decline. In the following, we elucidate the role of different kinds of processes associating with cluster decline: lock-in, the exit of an anchor firm, globalization, and life-cycle phases.

Lock-in

Lock-in (Belussi and Sedita 2009; Blažek et al. 2020) is arguably the most popular conceptual frame for explaining cluster decline.[5] Menzel and Fornahl (2010) synthetize the typical use of lock-in in the evolutionary oriented cluster literature:

> The former clustering advantages may turn into disadvantages as the clustered companies become locked into a trajectory that once marked their success, but is not able to cope with contemporary development.
>
> (p. 208)

The idea here is that, as in all evolutionary processes, specialization and accompanied learning strengthen a cluster for certain type of competition and institutional setting yet lose this advantage if the environment changes (Hassink and Shin 2005; Popp and Wilson 2007). Understood this way, lock-in resembles imprinting (Simsek, Fox and Heavey 2015) and deglomeration (Weber 1909). Overall, most of the literature that uses lock-in as an important concept uses it in rather liberal ways (see especially Popp and Wilson 2007). Some studies explicitly link lock-in to the larger scientific discourse on path dependence (Isaksen and Trippl 2014), while others take lock-in as a more metaphorical reference to a situation in which a cluster faces difficulties in renewal (e.g., Coenen, Moodysson and Martin 2015; Trippl and Otto 2009).

Two most common types of lock-in in the literature we reviewed are technological and institutional.[6] Technological lock-in refers to historically accumulated skills and knowledge which do not fit a new equilibrium. Examples of lock-in into inferior technologies are Østergaard and Park's (2015) study of wireless communication cluster in Denmark, Parsons and Rose's (2005) study of the Lancashire cotton industry, and Lamberg and colleagues' (2021) study of Finland's mobile phone cluster. These and similar studies report processes in which the adaptation speed at the factory level is much slower than global changes in technology, the end-result being a loss of competitiveness. At the same time, we have also identified studies in which a historically accumulated technological competence does not prevent decline but slows down the process, potentially creating opportunities for renewal. Such studies are, for example, Hassink's (2007) study of German textile industry, Treado's (2010) study of Pittsburgh steel industry, and Vanthillo and colleagues' (2018) study of the chemical complex around Antwerp Port. A common theme in these studies is the value of accumulated knowledge and reputation that prevents a collapse and helps to buy time for renewal.

Another group of studies uses lock-in to reflect a broader state of stagnation – not only in technology or competences – but also in terms of institutions (Hassink and Shin 2005; Wenting and Frenken 2011), cognitive frames (Porac, Thomas and Baden-Fuller 1989), and culture (Isaksen 2018). In some studies, a sociocultural lock-in is seen as an antecedent of decline. A classic example is the Scottish knitwear industry studied by Porac, Thomas and Baden-Fuller (1989) (which would now be defined as a cluster or ecosystem) in which a biased cognition on the competitiveness prevented renewal and resulted in decline. Similarly, Isaksen (2018) studies conventions as inhibiting change; Bellandi and Santini (2017) studied how established cognitions and institutional frames result in the lack of adaptability and low resilience, and Wenting and Frenken (2011) studied how the imbalance between maintenance of local legitimacy and global competition processes cause relative decline.

Anchor firm

Not all clusters and ecosystems are 'Silicon Valley – like' emphasizing shared business services, labor supply, network dynamics, coopetition, and other factors originating in co-location (Saxenian 1996). Instead, some clusters are built upon a dominant firm that drives the development of smaller firms by creating demand for specialized services and businesses (Gray, Golob and Markusen 1996). Taken as ecosystems, symbiosis around one or a few larger firms is obligatory in a sense that the absence of a 'hub' (idem.) kills or harms other firms and organizations whereas locations characterized by a large number of firms benefiting from co-location the going and coming of new organization do not affect the survival of the cluster (Saxenian 2007). Accordingly, the exit (by change of location or dissolution) of an anchor firm is a common reason for cluster decline in hub-and-spoke clusters and ecosystems.

The literature we use sees the influence of anchor firms in cluster evolution in two main ways. The first and more obvious emphasizes the risks associated with a powerful anchor firm. For example, Engelen and Grote (2009) examine the virtualization of anchor firms in finance industry finding that the fading of an anchor firms from some specific geographical locations has severe consequences for smaller, second-tier finance centers. Likewise, Randelli and Lombardi (2014) find the gatekeeper role of anchor firms as harmful for the existence of variation and new business generation in an Italian textile industry cluster.

The second related theme originates in multinational corporations, which many studies (e.g., Denney, Southin and Wolfe 2020; Livi and Jeannerat 2015; Østergaard and Park 2015) identify as threats to cluster vitality (and thus a mechanism in cluster decline if they make an exit). Østergaard and Park (2015) and Østergaard and Reinau (2016), for example, report on how the entry and subsequent exit of a multinational telecommunication firm drove a cluster toward decline. Overall, the entry and exit connotate both potential positive and negative consequences, yet in both cases the propensity of a cluster to drift toward decline depends on the existence of variation among the smaller 'spoke' firms and supporting organizations like universities (Mudambi et al. 2017) and local public organizations (Martin, Mayer and Mayneris 2011).

Globalization

Earlier review studies of industry decline have found globalization and more generally the rise of other more competitive regions as a major reason for the decline of local industrial districts (Lamberg, Ojala and Peltoniemi 2018). The same applies to clusters and ecosystems. Yet, the results from empirical and case-based studies are much less homogenous. The basic explanatory logic in globalization affecting cluster decline is of two kinds. First is the effect of new competition originating in the global market (Zucchella 2006), typically as a consequence of new clusters somewhere else where factor endowments are more cost-effective (Hassink and Shin 2005). The second concerns the exit of anchor firms – effectively running behind the lesser costs and more lucrative markets (Østergaard and Park 2015).

The literature we have studied reports several cases in which globalization has driven a cluster to decline in furniture industry (Amdam and Bjarnar 2015), gold jewelry (De Marchi, Lee and Gereffi 2014), French fashion industry (Wenting and Frenken 2011), or film production in Hollywood (Christopherson 2013). The results, however, emphasize the heterogeneity of reasons and consequences of globalization. Wenting and Frenken (2011), for example, show how legitimization processes at the local level hindered the French fashion industry's opportunities to transform in response to challenges originating in a new competitive regime operating globally. Likewise, Amdam and Bjarnar (2015) report in their study of Norwegian furniture and boat clusters how the former cluster failed to become globally competitive while the latter eventually reached a global leadership position. Christopherson (2013) similarly finds that some firms in the Hollywood film production cluster benefited from the globalization of their customer base while others suffered. Accordingly, globalization drives clusters in varying directions and may also enhance heterogeneity among cluster organizations.

Some studies would also predict a more fundamental change in cluster competition. Saxenian's most recent work (2007) argues for new types of interregional (and thus intercluster) ties when immigrants working in Silicon Valley companies move to other locations with their knowledge and personal ties allowing cluster-like development across geographic locations. We have also studies showing that globalization may increase the power of bottleneck companies in global value networks (Jacobides and Tae 2015) potentially resulting in the collapse or decline of geographically centered clusters. Järvinen, Lamberg and Pietinalho (2012), for example, demonstrate with a longitudinal network analysis how the rising importance of two key technology providers resulted in almost total collapse of a regional paper and pulp industry clusters.

Life cycle

Drawing from the broader industry life-cycle literature (see chapter two), clusters have also been theorized to develop through life cycles that include the stages of emergence, growth, sustainment, and decline (Menzel and Fornahl 2010). Life-cycle logic, with a distinct decline stage, has also been theorized to apply to different types of clusters such as industrial districts (De Propris and Lazzeretti 2009; Popp and Wilson 2007) and entrepreneurial ecosystems (Cantner et al. 2021). To get an overview of how cluster life cycle develops through different stages, Menzel and Fornahl (2010) write:

> As the cluster emerges, there are only a few companies and the heterogeneity increases strongly because every new company ventures into new technological areas of the cluster. In the growth phase, the technological path becomes increasingly focused. The heterogeneity decreases until the cluster has matured and a distinct development path has taken shape. However, if the cluster is focused too narrowly, it loses its capacity for renewal and declines.
>
> (p. 218)

Building on this, the decline stage of cluster life cycle is characterized by the decrease in the number of companies and employees (due to business failures and rationalization), while the cluster becomes locked in to technology paths/traditions and ceases to produce variation through the creation of new knowledge and entry by start-up companies (Menzel and Fornahl 2010). This is often accompanied by declining demand for the goods that the cluster produces (De Propris and Lazzeretti 2009; Elola et al. 2012). For instance, De Propris and Lazzeretti (2009) recount how the Birmingham Jewelry Quarter faced slow decline due to replacement by foreign imports, inability to find new market opportunities, and a slow decline in labor and firm density.

The decline process and the accompanying specialization also make clusters susceptible to the disruptive effects of new technologies. For instance, Dalum, Pedersen and Villumsen (2005) recount how the development of first- and second-generation mobile phone technologies led to the emergence of a NorCOM wireless communication cluster in the North Jutland region of Denmark but the development of third-generation mobile phone technology presented a significant threat to the cluster as it requires financial investments that exceed the capacity of the companies in that cluster. Yet, the decline stage of the cluster life cycle does not need to be a terminal state since clusters can also find a path of renewal that can lead them out of the state of decline (e.g., Cantner et al. 2021; Menzel and Fornahl 2010).

How cluster decline can be managed

Menzel and Fornahl (2010) offer three possible ways of managing decline: (1) "the cluster simply diminishes"; (2) adding new technologies to enhance efficiency and possibilities to reach an enhanced competitiveness; or (3) transition to new fields of business. We add to these notions by observing managerial opportunities from a two-dimensional matrix in Figure 3.2.

The dimensions of the matrix are the dependence of an anchor firm and the degree of policy interventions along the life cycle of the cluster. The reasoning is as follows. Most of the decline- and collapse-eliciting factors operate across clusters: lock-in happens almost automatically in conjunction with cluster tenure, location is very difficult to change, globalization affects all clusters somehow, and the weakening dynamics of interorganizational ties is as much outcome as an antecedent. In contrast, our review highlights the strong influence of anchor firm on the livelihood of clusters, and from earlier theoretical and empirical literature we know the impact of policy intervention magnitude on cluster competitiveness. Accordingly, combining these perspectives allows us to add nuances to Menzel and Fornahl's suggestions.

Concerning the suggestions listed in our matrix, the role of state or other public sector actors appears central in the management of decline especially yet not only in planning-based clusters (Su and Hung 2009). The repertoire of

	Anchor firm impact	
	Strong	**Weak**
Emergent market dynamics	*Typical challenge:* anchor firm makes an exit *Managerial responses:* (a) enhancement of interfirm ties by attracting new firm entry through infrastructure investments (universities, venture capital availability, etc.); and (b) investment into cluster-level innovation processes.	*Typical challenge:* the cluster loses international competitiveness *Managerial responses:* (a) an orchestrated effort to renew by focusing on previously secondary business areas and (b) specific public support mechanisms to facilitate the transform from the old to the new.
Planning and policy choices	*Typical challenge:* anchor firm makes an exit (oftentimes after it has been lured to invest with public subsidies) *Managerial responses:* (a) preventing the exit by promising more money and other subsidies; (b) investing into the existing businesses with the hope of renewal; or (c) terminal care.	*Typical challenge:* the cluster loses its competitiveness due to globalization, suboptimal location, and other reasons *Managerial responses:* (a) investing into existing businesses while simultaneously creating infrastructure in the forms of universities and other R&D intensive organizations; or (b) terminal care.

(Row group label: **Born and developed by**)

Figure 3.2 Managerial opportunities regarding cluster decline

possible actions goes in two directions: to prevent the shrinking of a cluster or managing the end of clusters in societally sustainable way. Both ways require money and other resources (Martin, Mayer and Mayneris 2011). By terminal care we mean investments in unemployment management, preventing pollution and other environment threats resulting from the end of industrial production, transforming business districts into residential areas, and other activities necessary after the cluster approaches or enters its terminal phase (Hudson 1994). If the public authorities decide to save the cluster, they may try to attract an anchor firm (or replace it with a similar firm). In this connection, the transformation from decline to renewal may also require a dedicated support mechanism in the form of tax relief, for example, or investment in the cluster infrastructure in the form of universities or research laboratories (Bramwell and Wolfe 2008).

Some mechanisms assist with cluster renewal but require multistakeholder approaches (Roloff 2008) in which private and public actors *collaboratively* engage in actions (Amdam and Bjarnar 2015). For example, the enhancement of interorganizational ties may require orchestrated effort from venture capitalists (Sun et al. 2019), new business incubators, universities (Bramwell and Wolfe 2008), and local authorities (Swords 2013). Likewise, the enhancement of secondary businesses to replace earlier dominant businesses requires orchestrated effort to happen. Such processes and emergent finding of a new collaborative strategic directions are challenging but doable with a healthy core of competent firms and organizations.

Summary

This chapter provided an overview of research on cluster and ecosystem decline and how that decline can be managed. We have again focused on what constitutes decline, what causes decline, what happens during decline, and how decline can be managed.

To answer *what constitutes decline*, we have outlined two classes of decline and their central indicators. These two classes cover different ways in which a cluster can experience decline:

1 Losing competitiveness compared to global competition
2 Losing an ability to engage in renewal

To understand how clusters can end up in a state of decline, we have examined *what causes cluster decline*. We identify three causes of cluster decline:

1 Factor endowments (especially deteriorating benefits accrued by a location; dwindling natural resources; labor costs and availability; and lack and/or wrong timing of venture capital)

2   Knowledge and capabilities (especially turning them into rigidities; con-
     centration increasing internal competition; and co-dependent decline of
     different capabilities)
3   Interorganizational dynamics (lack of employee mobility and buzz;
     decreasing social capital)

Thereafter, we examined *what happens during cluster decline* by analyzing
a set of decline processes we identified from the literature. Lock-in originates from the literature on path dependence and explains decline as an
increasing narrowness in terms of business foci and institutionalized ways
of interpreting competitive advantage in the cluster. Also, lock-in refers
to high transformation costs even if decision-makers have a motivation to
engage in renewal. The exit of an anchor firm is almost purely an empirical
construct (although also an analogy from biological research on symbiotic
populations). The exit of an anchor firm seriously harms and even destroys
clusters that are excessively dependent on the anchor firm(s). Globalization affects cluster in through competition (concerning both products and
resources), firms' location decisions, and public policies (trade policy, taxes,
support mechanisms). Finally, life-cycle explanations concern both cluster
life cycles (including a host of related factors like lock-in) and industry life
cycles affecting cluster decline through deterioration at the industry level.
    Finally, we described *how decline can be managed* by public sector and as
multistakeholder projects. Public sector organizations' role is crucial in the
management of decline situations yet especially the ecosystem and industrial
district literatures also emphasize the importance of multistakeholder projects in which actors from entrepreneurs to universities and public authorities
together look for a course of action (whether renewal or exit). Collectively,
the following actions are prevalent when managing cluster decline:

*   Enhancements of interfirm ties by attracting new firm entry
*   Investments into cluster-level innovation processes
*   Focusing on previously marginal business areas
*   Activation of public support mechanisms to bridge the transformation
    from the old to the new
*   Preventing firm exits by promising money and other subsidies
*   Investing more into the existing businesses with a hope of renewal
*   Terminal care: facilitating the end of a cluster with minimum social and
    environmental costs

Taken together, these analyses allow the reader to identify the reasons for
cluster decline, analyze what the decline process will likely mean, and what
strategic options there are for adapting to decline. These takeaways are
summarized in Figure 3.3.

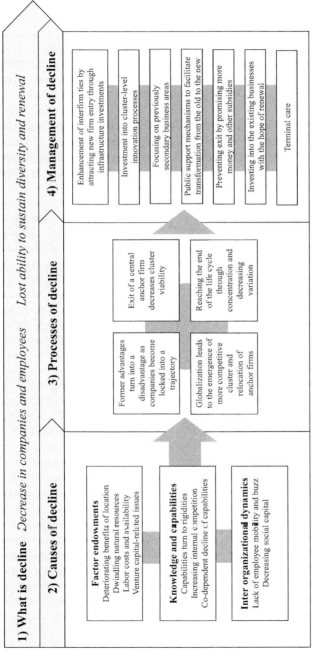

Figure 3.3 Integrative framework of cluster decline research

Further reading suggestions

To understand the role and the causes of cluster decline embedded in cluster evolution, we suggest reading Menzel and Fornahl's (2010) work as an excellent starting point.

- Menzel, M. P., & Fornahl, D. (2010). Cluster life cycles – Dimensions and rationales of cluster evolution. *Industrial and Corporate Change*, 19(1), 205–238. DOI: 10.1093/icc/dtp036

We built extensively on theoretical work of economic geographers. The influential research of Martin and Sunley (2003), Hassink (2016), and Markusen (1996b) helps to reflect the normative suggestions by Porter and other proponents of the cluster approach against the much longer historical tradition in the study of industry agglomerations.

- Martin, R., & Sunley, P. (2003). Deconstructing clusters: Chaotic concept or policy panacea? *Journal of Economic Geography*, 3(1), 5–35. DOI: 10.1093/jeg/3.1.5
- Hassink, R. (2016). Cluster decline and political lock-ins. *Unfolding Cluster Evolution* (eds. Fiorenza Belussi & Jose Luis Hervás-Oliver). London: Routledge.
- Markusen, A. (1996). Sticky places in slippery space: A typology of industrial districts. *Economic Geography*, 72(3), 293–313. DOI: 10.2307/144402

Another perspective concerns the meta-theoretical underpinnings of cluster and ecosystem approaches. Teece (2007) and Jacobides and Tae (2015) add excellent viewpoints to the economic logic on clusters and ecosystems, and Sydow, Schreyögg and Koch (2009) add to the understanding of the path-dependent logic of cluster evolution.

- Sydow, J., Schreyögg, G., & Koch, J. (2009). Organizational path dependence: Opening the black box. *Academy of Management Review*, 34(4), 689–709.
- Teece, D. J. (2007). Explicating dynamic capabilities: The nature and microfoundations of (sustainable) enterprise performance. *Strategic Management Journal*, 28(13), 1319–1350. DOI: 10.1002/smj.640
- Jacobides, M. G., & Tae, C. J. (2015). Kingpins, bottlenecks, and value dynamics along a sector. *Organization Science*, 26(3), 889–907. DOI: 10.1287/orsc.2014.0958

Finally, to reach a strategic and future-oriented outlook on the management of clusters and ecosystems, we suggest Saxenian (2007) for an enhanced understanding of the changing nature of location in intercluster competition and Rietveld, Schilling and Bellavitis (2019) on platform strategy.

- Saxenian, A. (2007). *The New Argonauts: Regional Advantage in a Global Economy*. Cambridge: Harvard University Press.
- Rietveld, J., Schilling, M. A., & Bellavitis, C. (2019). Platform strategy: Managing ecosystem value through selective promotion of complements. *Organization Science*, 30(6), 1232–1251. DOI: 10.1287/orsc.2019.1290

Notes

1 As Martin (1999) shows, there would be good reasons to avoid Porter's model and conceptualization or at least "the cluster concept should carry a public policy health warning" (Martin and Sunley, 2003: 5). We see "cluster" as an umbrella concept under which we focus on the decline phase of geographically concentrated firms and organizations having synergies and a shared identity while simultaneously avoiding the normative underpinnings.
2 For further delineation of the specific characteristics of platforms and the links between platforms and ecosystems, see Rietveld, Schilling and Bellavitis (2019) and Kim (2016).
3 There is also a dedicated literature on cluster-level resilience partly relevant also for our review. See, e.g., Hassink (2010b) and Christopherson, Michie and Tyler (2010).
4 Porter (1990), echoing a long tradition in industrial organization, listed factor conditions, demand conditions, related and supporting industries, firm strategy, structure and rivalry, and government and chance events to be relevant for the vitality of clusters.
5 For more exhaustive treatment of the concept, see Sydow, Schreyögg and Koch (2009), Page (2006), and Mahoney (2000).
6 Hassink and Shin (2015), building on Grabher (1993), categorize lock-in in functional, cognitive, and political types, which may be seen as overlapping with our focus on technological and cognitive-cultural lock-in. The Hassink and Shin categories, neither the Popp and Wilson (2007) systemic category, did not, however, emerge inductively from the texts we analyzed, and we decided to use a more inductive approach in this context.

References

Amdam, R. P., & Bjarnar, O. (2015). Globalization and the development of industrial clusters: Comparing two Norwegian clusters, 1900–2010. *Business History Review*, 89(4), 693–413. https://doi.org/10.1017/S0007680515001051

Atta-Mills, J., Alder, J., & Rashid Sumaila, U. (2004) The decline of a regional fishing nation: The case of Ghana and West Africa. *Natural Resources Forum, 28*(1), 13–21. https://doi.org/10.1111/j.0165-0203.2004.00068.x

Audretsch, D. B., & Feldman, M. P. (1996). R&D spillovers and the geography of innovation and production. *The American Economic Review, 86*(3), 630–640.

Auerswald, P. E., & Dani, L. (2017). The adaptive life cycle of entrepreneurial ecosystems: The biotechnology cluster. *Small Business Economics, 49*(1), 97–117. https://doi.org/10.1007/s11187-017-9869-3

Bathelt, H., Malmberg, A., & Maskell, P. (2004). Clusters and knowledge: Local buzz, global pipelines and the process of knowledge creation. *Progress in Human Geography, 28*(1), 31–56. https://doi.org/10.1191/0309132504ph469oa

Baum, T. (1999). The decline of the traditional North Atlantic Fisheries and Tourism's Response: The cases of Iceland and Newfoundland. *Current Issues in Tourism, 2*(1), 47–67. https://doi.org/10.1080/13683509908667843

Becattini, G. (2017). The Marshallian industrial district as a socio-economic notion. *Revue d'économie Industrielle, 157*(1), 13–32.

Begg, I. (1999). Cities and competitiveness. *Urban Studies, 36*(5–6), 795–809. https://doi.org/10.1080/0042098993222

Bellandi, M., & Santini, E. (2017). Resilience and the role of arts and culture-based activities in mature industrial districts. *European Planning Studies, 25*(1), 88–106. https://doi.org/10.1080/09654313.2016.1268096

Belussi, F., & Hervas-Oliver, J. L. (Eds.). (2016). *Unfolding Cluster Evolution.* London: Routledge.

Belussi, F., & Sedita, S. R. (2009). Life cycle vs. multiple path dependency in industrial districts. *European Planning Studies, 17*(4), 505–528. https://doi.org/10.1080/09654310802682065

Blažek, J., Květoň, V., Baumgartinger-Seiringer, S., & Trippl, M. (2020). The dark side of regional industrial path development: Towards a typology of trajectories of decline. *European Planning Studies, 28*(8), 1455–1473. https://doi.org/10.1080/09654313.2019.1685466

Blim, M. L. (1990). Economic development and decline in the emerging global factory: Some Italian lessons. *Politics and Society, 18*(1), 143–163. https://doi.org/10.1177/003232929001800106

Boschma, R., & Fornahl, D. (2011). Cluster evolution and a roadmap for future research. *Regional Studies, 45*(10), 1295–1298. https://doi.org/10.1080/00343404.2011.633253

Bramwell, A., & Wolfe, D. A. (2008). Universities and regional economic development: The entrepreneurial University of Waterloo. *Research Policy, 37*(8), 1175–1187. https://doi.org/10.1016/j.respol.2008.04.016

Brenner, T. (2004). *Local Industrial Clusters: Existence, Emergence and Evolution.* London: Routledge.

Bresnahan, T., & Gambardella, A. (Eds.). (2004). *Building High-Tech Clusters: Silicon Valley and Beyond.* Cambridge: Cambridge University Press.

Bresnahan, T., Gambardella, A., & Saxenian, A. (2001). "Old economy" inputs for "new economy" outcomes: Cluster formation in the new Silicon Valleys. *Industrial and Corporate Change, 10*(4), 835–860. https://doi.org/10.1093/icc/10.4.835

Brunello, G., & Langella, M. (2016). Local agglomeration, entrepreneurship and the 2008 recession: Evidence from Italian industrial districts. *Regional Science and Urban Economics*, *58*, 104–114. https://doi.org/10.1016/j.regsciurbeco.2016.03.004

Brusco, S. (1982). The Emilian model: Productive decentralisation and social integration. *Cambridge Journal of Economics*, *6*(2), 167–184. https://doi.org/10.1093/oxfordjournals.cje.a035506

Cantner, U., Cunningham, J. A., Lehmann, E. E., & Menter, M. (2021). Entrepreneurial ecosystems: A dynamic lifecycle model. *Small Business Economics*, *57*(1), 407–423. https://doi.org/10.1007/s11187-020-00316-0

Christopherson, S. (2013). Hollywood in decline? US film and television producers beyond the era of fiscal crisis. *Cambridge Journal of Regions, Economy and Society*, *6*(1), 141–157. https://doi.org/10.1093/cjres/rss024

Christopherson, S., Michie, J., & Tyler, P. (2010). Regional resilience: Theoretical and empirical perspectives. *Cambridge Journal of Regions, Economy and Society*, *3*(1), 3–10. https://doi.org/10.1093/cjres/rsq004

Coenen, L., Moodysson, J., & Martin, H. (2015). Path renewal in old industrial regions: Possibilities and limitations for regional innovation policy. *Regional Studies*, *49*(5), 850–865. https://doi.org/10.1080/00343404.2014.979321

Dalum, B., Pedersen, C. Ø., & Villumsen, G. (2005). Technological life-cycles: lessons from a cluster facing disruption. *European Urban and Regional Studies*, *12*(3), 229–246. https://doi.org/10.1177/0969776405056594

De Marchi, V., Lee, J., & Gereffi, G. (2014). Globalization, recession and the internationalization of industrial districts: Experiences from the Italian gold jewellery industry. *European Planning Studies*, *22*(4), 866–884. https://doi.org/10.1080/09654313.2013.771624

Denney, S., Southin, T., & Wolfe, D. A. (2021). Entrepreneurs and cluster evolution: The transformation of Toronto's ICT cluster. *Regional Studies*, *55*(2), 196–207. https://doi.org/10.1080/00343404.2020.1762854

De Propris, L., & Lazzeretti, L. (2009). Measuring the decline of a Marshallian industrial district: The Birmingham jewellery quarter. *Regional Studies*, *43*(9), 1135–1154. https://doi.org/10.1080/00343400802070894

Desmarchelier, B., & Zhang, L. (2018). Innovation networks and cluster dynamics. *The Annals of Regional Science*, *61*(3), 553–578. https://doi.org/10.1007/s00168-018-0882-5

Einarsson, N. (2009). From good to eat to good to watch: Whale watching, adaptation and change in Icelandic fishing communities. *Polar Research*, *28*(1), 129–138. https://doi.org/10.1111/j.1751-8369.2008.00092.x

Elola, A., Valdaliso, J., López, S. & Aranguren, MJ. (2012). Cluster Life Cycles, Path Dependency and Regional Economic Development: Insights from a Meta-Study on Basque Clusters, European Planning Studies, 20:2, 257–279, DOI: 10.1080/09654313.2012.650902

Engelen, E., & Grote, M. H. (2009). Stock exchange virtualisation and the decline of second-tier financial centres – The cases of Amsterdam and Frankfurt. *Journal of Economic Geography*, *9*(5), 679–696. https://doi.org/10.1093/jeg/lbp027

Gertler, M. S. (1996). Worlds apart: The changing market geography of the German machinery industry. *Small Business Economics*, *8*(2), 87–106. https://doi.org/10.1007/BF00394420

Gittell, R., & Sohl, J. (2005). Technology centres during the economic downturn: What have we learned? *Entrepreneurship and Regional Development, 17*(4), 293–312. https://doi.org/10.1080/08985620500202582

Gordon, I. R., & McCann, P. (2000). Industrial clusters: Complexes, agglomeration and/or social networks? *Urban Studies, 37*(3), 513–532. https://doi.org/10.1080/0042098002096

Grabher, G. (1993). The weakness of strong ties: The lock-in of regional development in the Ruhr area. In G. Grabher (Ed.), *The Embedded Firm: On the Socio-economics of Industrial Networks* (pp. 255–277). London: Routledge.

Gray, M., Golob, E., & Markusen, A. (1996). Big firms, long arms, wide shoulders: The "hub-and-spoke" industrial district in the Seattle region. *Regional Studies, 30*(7), 651–666. https://doi.org/10.1080/00343409612331349948

Haber, S., Maurer, N., & Razo, A. (2003). When the law does not matter: The rise and decline of the Mexican Oil Industry. *The Journal of Economic History, 63*(1), 1–32. https://doi.org/10.1017/S0022050703001712

Hannigan, T. J., Cano-Kollmann, M., & Mudambi, R. (2015). Thriving innovation amidst manufacturing decline: The Detroit auto cluster and the resilience of local knowledge production. *Industrial and Corporate Change, 24*(3), 613–634. https://doi.org/10.1093/icc/dtv014

Harrison, B. (1992). Industrial districts: Old wine in new bottles? *Regional Studies, 26*(5), 469–483. https://doi.org/10.1080/00343400701232264

Hassink, R. (2007). The strength of weak lock-ins: The renewal of the Westmünsterland textile industry. *Environment and Planning A, 39*(5), 1147–1165. https://doi.org/10.1068/a3848

Hassink, R. (2010a). Locked in decline? On the role of regional lock-ins in old industrial areas. In Ron Boschma & Ron Martin (Eds.), *The Handbook of Evolutionary Economic Geography*. London: Edward Elgar.

Hassink, R. (2010b). Regional resilience: A promising concept to explain differences in regional economic adaptability? *Cambridge Journal of Regions, Economy and Society, 3*(1), 45–58. https://doi.org/10.1093/cjres/rsp033

Hassink, R. (2016). Cluster decline and political lock-ins. In Fiorenza Belussi & Jose Luis Hervás-Oliver (Eds.), *Unfolding Cluster Evolution*. London: Routledge.

Hassink, R., & Shin, D. H. (2005). The restructuring of old industrial areas in Europe and Asia. *Environment and Planning A, 37*(4), 571–580. https://doi.org/10.1068/a36273

Hausmann, R., & Neffke, F. M. (2019). The workforce of pioneer plants: The role of worker mobility in the diffusion of industries. *Research Policy, 48*(3), 628–648. https://doi.org/10.1016/j.respol.2018.10.017

Hudson, R. (1994). Institutional change, cultural transformation, and economic regeneration: Myths and realities from Europe's old industrial areas. In A. Amin & N. Thrift (Eds.), *Globalization, Institutions, and Regional Development in Europe*. Oxford: Oxford University Press.

Isaksen, A., & Trippl, M. (2014). Regional industrial path development in different regional innovation systems: A conceptual analysis. *Papers in Innovation Studies* 2014/17, Lund University, CIRCLE – Centre for Innovation Research.

Isaksen, A. (2018). From success to failure, the disappearance of clusters: a study of a Norwegian boat-building cluster. *Cambridge Journal of Regions, Economy and Society, 11*(2): 241–255, https://doi.org/10.1093/cjres/rsy007

Jacobides, M. G., & Tae, C. J. (2015). Kingpins, bottlenecks, and value dynamics along a sector. *Organization Science, 26*(3), 889–907. https://doi.org/10.1287/orsc.2014.0958

Järvinen, J., Lamberg, J.-A., & Pietinalho, L. (2012). The fall and the fragmentation of national clusters: Cluster evolution in the paper and pulp industry. *Journal of Forest Economics, 18*(3), 218–241. https://doi.org/10.1016/j.jfe.2012.04.002

Kabisch, N., Haase, D., & Haase, A. (2012). Urban population development in Europe, 1991–2008: The examples of Poland and the UK. *International Journal of Urban and Regional Research, 36*(6), 1326–1348. https://doi.org/10.1111/j.1468-2427.2012.01114.x

Kim, J. (2016). The platform business model and business ecosystem: Quality management and revenue structures. *European Planning Studies, 24*(12), 2113–2132. https://doi.org/10.1080/09654313.2016.1251882

Klepper, S. (2016). *Experimental Capitalism: The Nanoeconomics of American High-tech Industries.* Princeton: Princeton University Press.

Knight, E., Kumar, V., Wójcik, D., & O'Neill, P. (2020). The competitive advantage of regions: Economic geography and strategic management intersections. *Regional Studies, 54*(5), 591–595. https://doi.org/10.1080/00343404.2020.1739262

Kourtit, K., & Nijkamp, P. (2013). In praise of megacities in a global world. *Regional Science Policy and Practice, 5*(2), 167–182. https://doi.org/10.1111/rsp3.12002

Lamberg, J. A., Lubinaitė, S., Ojala, J., & Tikkanen, H. (2021). The curse of agility: The Nokia Corporation and the loss of market dominance in mobile phones, 2003–2013. *Business History, 63*(4), 574–605. https://doi.org/10.1080/00076791.2019.1593964

Lamberg, J. A., Ojala, J., & Peltoniemi, M. (2018). Thinking about industry decline: A qualitative meta-analysis and future research directions. *Business History, 60*(2), 127–156. https://doi.org/10.1080/00076791.2017.1340943

Leonard-Barton, D. (1992). Core capabilities and core rigidities: A paradox in managing new product development. *Strategic Management Journal, 13*(S1), 111–125. https://doi.org/10.1002/smj.4250131009

Livi, C., & Jeannerat, H. (2015). Born to be sold: Start-ups as products and new territorial life cycles of industrialization. *European Planning Studies, 23*(10), 1953–1974. https://doi.org/10.1080/09654313.2014.960180

Mahoney, J. (2000). Path dependence in historical sociology. *Theory and Society, 29*(4), 507–548. https://doi.org/10.1023/A:1007113830879

Markusen, A. (1996a). Interaction between regional and industrial policies: Evidence from four countries. *International Regional Science Review, 19*(1–2), 49–77. https://doi.org/10.1177/016001769601900205

Markusen, A. (1996b). Sticky places in slippery space: A typology of industrial districts. *Economic Geography, 72*(3), 293–313. https://doi.org/10.2307/144402

Martin, P., Mayer, T., & Mayneris, F. (2011). Public support to clusters: A firm level study of French "Local productive systems." *Regional Science and Urban Economics, 41*(2), 108–123. https://doi.org/10.1016/j.regsciurbeco.2010.09.001

Martin, R. (1999). The new "geographical turn" in economics: Some critical reflections. *Cambridge Journal of Economics, 23*(1), 65–91.

Martin, R., & Sunley, P. (2003). Deconstructing clusters: Chaotic concept or policy panacea? *Journal of Economic Geography, 3*(1), 5–35. https://doi.org/10.1093/jeg/3.1.5

Mattsson, J. T. (2008). *Organizational Diversity and Industry Evolution: The Entry of Modern Biotechnology Firms in Finland 1973–2006.* Espoo: Helsinki University of Technology.

Menzel, M. P., & Fornahl, D. (2010). Cluster life cycles – Dimensions and rationales of cluster evolution. *Industrial and Corporate Change, 19*(1), 205–238. https://doi.org/10.1093/icc/dtp036

Moen, E. (1998). *The Decline of the Pulp and Paper Industry in Norway, 1950–1980. A Study of a Closed System in an Open Economy.* Oslo: Scandinavian University Press.

Mossig, I. (2011). Regional employment growth in the cultural and creative industries in Germany 2003–2008. *European Planning Studies, 19*(6), 967–990. https://doi.org/10.1080/09654313.2011.568807

Mossig, I., & Schieber, L. (2016). Driving forces of cluster evolution – Growth and lock-in of two German packaging machinery clusters. *European Urban and Regional Studies, 23*(4), 594–611. https://doi.org/10.1177/0969776414536061

Mudambi, R., Mudambi, S. M., Mukherjee, D., & Scalera, V. G. (2017). Global connectivity and the evolution of industrial clusters: From tires to polymers in Northeast Ohio. *Industrial Marketing Management, 61*(1), 20–29. https://doi.org/10.1016/j.indmarman.2016.07.007

Naldi, L., Larsson, J. P., & Westlund, H. (2020). Policy entrepreneurship and entrepreneurial orientation in vulnerable Swedish municipalities. *Entrepreneurship and Regional Development, 32*(7–8), 473–491. https://doi.org/10.1080/08985626.2020.1798557

Nykänen, N. (2018). Competing institutional logics in Soviet industrial location policy. *Eurasian Geography and Economics, 59*(3–4), 314–339. https://doi.org/10.1080/15387216.2019.1581631

Østergaard, C. R., & Park, E. (2015). What makes clusters decline? A study on disruption and evolution of a high-tech cluster in Denmark. *Regional Studies, 49*(5), 834–849. https://doi.org/10.1080/00343404.2015.1015975

Østergaard, C. R., & Reinau, K. (2016). The dual role of multinational corporations in cluster evolution: When you dance with the devil, you wait for the song to stop. In Fiorenza Belussi & Jose Luis Hervás-Oliver (Eds.), *Unfolding Cluster Evolution.* London: Routledge.

Page, S. E. (2006). Path dependence. *Quarterly Journal of Political Science, 1*(1), 87–115. https://doi.org/10.1561/100.00000006

Parsons, M., & Rose, M. B. (2005). The neglected legacy of Lancashire cotton: Industrial clusters and the U.K. outdoor trade, 1960–1990. *Enterprise and Society, 6*(4), 682–709. https://doi.org/10.1017/s1467222700015299

Peltoniemi, M. (2006). Preliminary theoretical framework for the study of business ecosystems. *Emergence: Complexity and Organization, 8*(1), 10–19.

Piper, L. (2010). Parasites from "alien shores": The decline of Canada's freshwater fishing industry. *Canadian Historical Review, 91*(1), 87–114. https://doi.org/10.3138/chr.91.1.87

Popp, A., & Wilson, J. (2007). Life cycles, contingency, and agency: Growth, development, and change in English industrial districts and clusters. *Environment and Planning A, 39*(12), 2975–2992. https://doi.org/10.1068/a38403

Porac, J. F., Thomas, H., & Baden-Fuller, C. (1989). Competitive groups as cognitive communities: The case of Scottish knitwear manufacturers. *Journal of Management Studies, 26*(4), 397–416. https://doi.org/10.1111/j.1467-6486.1989.tb00736.x

Porter, M. E. (1990). *The Competitive Advantage of Nations.* New York: Macmillan.

Porter, M. E. (2000). Location, competition, and economic development: Local clusters in a global economy. *Economic Development Quarterly, 14*(1), 15–34. https://doi.org/10.1177/089124240001400105

Porter, M. E. (2003). The Economic performance of regions. *Regional Studies, 37*(6–7), 549–578. https://doi.org/10.1080/0034340032000108688

Potter, A., & Watts, H. D. (2011). Evolutionary agglomeration theory: Increasing returns, diminishing returns, and the industry life cycle. *Journal of Economic Geography, 11*(3), 417–455. https://doi.org/10.1093/jeg/lbq004

Pyke, F., Becattini, G., & Sengenberger, W. (Eds.). (1990). *Industrial Districts and Inter-firm Co-operation in Italy.* Geneve: International Institute for Labour Studies.

Randelli, F., & Lombardi, M. (2014). The role of leading firms in the evolution of SME clusters: Evidence from the leather products cluster in Florence. *European Planning Studies, 22*(6), 1199–1211. https://doi.org/10.1080/09654313.2013.773963

Rietveld, J., Schilling, M. A., & Bellavitis, C. (2019). Platform strategy: Managing ecosystem value through selective promotion of complements. *Organization Science, 30*(6), 1232–1251. https://doi.org/10.1287/orsc.2019.1290

Roloff, J. (2008). Learning from Multi-Stakeholder Networks: Issue-Focussed Stakeholder Management. *Journal of Business Ethics* (82)3: 233–250 (2008). https://doi.org/10.1007/s10551-007-9573-3

Saxenian, A. (1983). The genesis of Silicon Valley. *Built Environment, 9*(1), 7–18.

Saxenian, A. (1996). *Regional Advantage: Culture and Competition in Silicon Valley and Route 128, with a New Preface by the Author.* Cambridge, MA: Harvard University Press.

Saxenian, A. (2007). *The New Argonauts: Regional Advantage in a Global Economy.* Cambridge, MA: Harvard University Press.

Simsek, Z., Fox, B. C., & Heavey, C. (2015). "What's past is prologue": A framework, review, and future directions for organizational research on imprinting. *Journal of Management, 41*(1), 288–317. https://doi.org/10.1177/0149206314553276

Su, Y. S., & Hung, L. C. (2009). Spontaneous vs. policy-driven: The origin and evolution of the biotechnology cluster. *Technological Forecasting and Social Change, 76*(5), 608–619. https://doi.org/10.1016/j.techfore.2008.08.008

Suire, R., & Vicente, J. (2009). Why do some places succeed when others decline? A social interaction model of cluster viability. *Journal of Economic Geography, 9*(3), 381–404. https://doi.org/10.1093/jeg/lbn053

Sun, S. L., Chen, V. Z., Sunny, S. A., & Chen, J. (2019). Venture capital as an innovation ecosystem engineer in an emerging market. *International Business Review, 28*(5), 101485. https://doi.org/10.1016/j.ibusrev.2018.02.012

Swords, J. (2013). Michael Porter's cluster theory as a local and regional development tool: The rise and fall of cluster policy in the UK. *Local Economy, 28*(4), 369–383. https://doi.org/10.1177/0269094213475855

Sydow, J., Schreyögg, G., & Koch, J. (2009). Organizational path dependence: Opening the black box. *Academy of Management Review, 34*(4), 689–709.

Teece, D. J. (2007). Explicating dynamic capabilities: The nature and microfoundations of (sustainable) enterprise performance. *Strategic Management Journal, 28*(13), 1319–1350. https://doi.org/10.1002/smj.640

Toivanen, H. (2004). *Learning and Corporate Strategy: The Dynamic Evolution of the North American Pulp and Paper Industry, 1860–1960* (Doctoral dissertation), Georgia Institute of Technology.

Tomlinson, P. R., & Branston, J. R. (2014). Turning the tide: Prospects for an industrial renaissance in the North Staffordshire ceramics industrial district. *Cambridge Journal of Regions, Economy and Society, 7*(3), 489–507. https://doi.org/10.1093/cjres/rsu016

Treado, C. D. (2010). Pittsburgh's evolving steel legacy and the steel technology cluster. *Cambridge Journal of Regions, Economy and Society, 3*(1), 105–120. https://doi.org/10.1093/cjres/rsp027

Trippl, M., Grillitsch, M., Isaksen, A., & Sinozic, T. (2015). Perspectives on cluster evolution: Critical review and future research issues. *European Planning Studies, 23*(10), 2028–2044. https://doi.org/10.1080/09654313.2014.999450

Trippl, M., & Otto, A. (2009). How to turn the fate of old industrial areas: A comparison of cluster-based renewal processes in Styria and the Saarland. *Environment and Planning A, 41*(5), 1217–1233. https://doi.org/10.1068/a4129

Vanthillo, T., Cant, J., Vanelslander, T., & Verhetsel, A. (2018). Understanding evolution in the Antwerp chemical cluster: The role of regional development strategies. *European Planning Studies, 26*(8), 1519–1536. https://doi.org/10.1080/09654313.2018.1491952

Vorley, T. (2008), The geographic cluster: A historical review. *Geography Compass, 2*, 790–813. https://doi.org/10.1111/j.1749-8198.2008.00108.x

Weber, A. (1909). *Über den Standort der Industrien, Vol. 1: Reine Theorie des Standorts; Mit Einem Mathematischen Anhang.* Tübingen: J. C. B. Mohr.

Wenting, R., & Frenken, K. (2011). Firm entry and institutional lock-in: An organizational ecology analysis of the global fashion design industry. *Industrial and Corporate Change, 20*(4), 1031–1048. https://doi.org/10.1093/icc/dtr032

Zucchella, A. (2006). Local cluster dynamics: Trajectories of mature industrial districts between decline and multiple embeddedness. *Journal of Institutional Economics, 2*(1), 21. https://doi.org/10.1017/S174413740500024X

4 Decline and failure at the organizational level

What constitutes organizational decline and failure

As with most concepts in social sciences, there is no commonly accepted definition of organizational decline. In their review, Mellahi and Wilkinson (2004, p. 22) state that several terms have been used in the literature: decline, bankruptcy, retrenchment, failure, downsizing, organization mortality, organizational death, and organizational exit. However, the most often-used label for organizational decline is *organizational failure*. It refers to the process through which something in the external and internal configurations of the organization makes it deteriorate and eventually fail. Here, organizational configurations can be defined as commonly occurring clusters of attributes of organizational strategies, structures, and processes (Miller 1981; Mintzberg 1979). Organizational decline research has therefore adopted the increasingly popular configurational approach that has made headway in strategy and organization research (see, e.g., Busenbark et al. 2016). If the organizational configuration is not right from the beginning (e.g., in the case of a start-up firm or a large greenfield investment to another country) or deteriorates due to external and internal reasons (e.g., when the top management of an incumbent firm fails to understand and react to the threat posed by new technological innovations introduced to the market by their competitors), organizational failure is imminent.

Despite numerous related terms and definitions, there seems to be a consensus on the meaning of organizational failure across research paradigms. In this chapter, we follow Cameron, Sutton and Whetten (1988), who define *organizational failure* as a:

> deterioration in an organization's adaptation to its microniche and the associated reduction of resources within the organization.
>
> (p. 9)

DOI: 10.4324/9781003035947-4

Due to the abundance of terminology and the close relationship between decline and failure, the terms *organizational decline* and *failure* are used interchangeably in this chapter. In doing so, they are taken to refer to the gradual deterioration of the configuration of the organization.

According to Mellahi and Wilkinson (2004), organizational failure has several underlying assumptions. First, failure has negative consequences, even though the final outcomes of failure may be positive, such as individual or organizational learning. Second, the definition does not *per se* specify the causes of organizational failure. The definition thus takes into consideration both intraorganizational and environmental factors. At the organizational level, it takes into account the psychological and organizational (e.g., structural and processual) characteristics that might cause organizations to decline and fail. Explanations of organizational decline and failure need thus to be searched among an array of environmental, ecological, organizational, and psychological factors. Finally, by extension, Ucbasaran et al. (2013) define *organizational failure* of an entrepreneurial firm as follows:

> [W]e define business failure as the cessation of involvement in a venture because it has not met a minimum threshold for economic viability as stipulated by the entrepreneur.
>
> (p. 175)

This definition therefore involves the following additional facet: the previous owners exit the focal business (through cessation of activities, a merger or an acquisition/takeover, or bankruptcy) which has not achieved a desired level of economic viability.

Decline can be located in any individual part, parts, or interlinkages in an organization's architecture and, to use a popular term, its business model. Smith, Binns and Tushman (2010, p. 450) define organizational architecture in terms of the "people, competencies, processes, culture and measurement systems" that enable an organization to run its business model, creating and appropriating value that the organization is designed to produce. Organizational architecture can also be related to the more traditional 'structuring of organizations' (Mintzberg 1979), meaning arriving at a structural configuration (e.g., a machine bureaucracy as an organizational archetype) as a function of the organizational design parameters (positions, superstructure, lateral linkages, and decision-making system) and the (mostly external) contingency factors (e.g., technology, political environment).

The result of decline can be a total exit from the market (by bankruptcy, merger, acquisition, or takeover, or by the cessation of operations) or a turnaround. In every case, there are several common symptoms for organization

Table 4.1 Symptoms of organizational decline and exemplary studies

Symptom of organizational decline	Exemplary studies
Shrinking financial resources	Cameron (1983)
Negative profitability	D'Aveni (1989), Hambrick and D'Aveni (1988)
Shrinking market	Harrigan (1982)
Loss of legitimacy	Benson (1975)
Exit from international markets	Burt et al. (2002), Jackson, Mellahi and Sparks (2005)
Severe market share erosion	Mellahi, Jackson and Sparks (2002), Starbuck, Greve and Hedberg (1978)

decline and failure. Consequently, Table 4.1 outlines some of the most common failure symptoms/indicators and studies that refer to these symptoms.

What causes organizational decline

In their review article, Mellahi and Wilkinson (2004, p. 27) provide an integrative framework of the determinants of organizational decline and failure (see Figure 4.1). The determinants fall in the categories of general

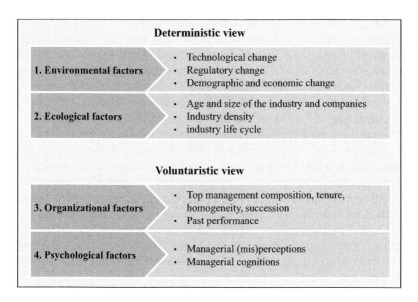

Figure 4.1 Causes of organizational decline according to Mellahi and Wilkinson (2004)

environmental factors (e.g., technological change, regulatory factors, demographic and economic change), ecological factors pertaining to the focal industry and companies therein (e.g., age, size, density, industry life cycle), organizational factors (e.g., top management composition and tenure, homogeneity, succession, past performance), and psychological factors (e.g., managerial (mis)perceptions and cognitions).

Mellahi and Wilkinson (2004) distinguished a strong bipolar situation at the turn of the millennium in terms of what was understood to cause decline. On the one hand, deterministic scholars such as population ecologists and industrial organization researchers studied firm failure mostly in terms of changing external conditions that define the fate of organizations. On the other hand, more research was conducted within the voluntaristic or 'strategic choice' paradigm, in which insufficient, lacking, or bluntly erroneous managerial strategic choices and actions were identified as the main reason for firm failure.

According to the recent review by Kücher and Feldbauer-Durstmüller (2019), the most-cited decline studies examined what went wrong in companies' adaptation processes (Hambrick and D'Aveni 1988), what organizational attributes are often found in declining firms (Cameron, Kim and Whetten 1987), what ultimately caused firms to fail, and why some firms survive phases of decline when others fail (D'Aveni 1989; Weitzel and Jonsson 1989). The review also provided a threefold framework to structure the current state of research to organizational decline (cf. the reviews by Mellahi and Wilkinson 2004, 2010; Ucbasaran et al. 2013). This framework is depicted in Figure 4.2.

Kücher and Feldbauer-Durstmüller (2019) identify a strong cluster of failure studies from a *deterministic perspective* that they label as "organizational ecology and industrial organization." These studies focused on quantitative analyses of a large number of emergent small firms in different industry and target country settings. This perspective dominated academic research on firm decline and failure especially from the early 1990s until the beginning of the new millennium. Its empirical objective is to uncover how environmental-ecological factors explain company decline and demise.

There are a diminishing number of studies from the *voluntaristic perspective*, often labeled "strategic choice." Here the failure of large established firms is studied with both quantitative and qualitative methods. In the voluntaristic paradigm, organizational learning-related perspectives have gained increasing attention since 2000. Most studies in this stream focus on the "in-house" psychological and organizational factors related to firm decline and failure. Kücher and Feldbauer-Durstmüller (2019) also argue that the first two traditional clusters of research have limited their attention to the reasons and processes that lead to failure in organizations.

Finally, there is the ever-more dominant *entrepreneurial perspective*, consisting of both deterministic and voluntaristic research approaches.

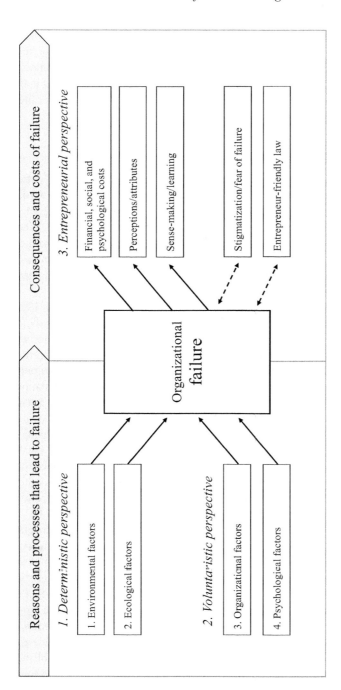

Figure 4.2 Structure of organizational decline and failure research. Adapted from Kücher and Feldbauer-Durstmüller (2019)

Reprinted from Journal of Business Research, 98, Kücher, A. & Feldbauer-Durstmüller, B., Organizational failure and decline - A bibliometric study of the scientific frontend, 503-516, 2019, with permission from Elsevier

Focusing on emergent small firms dominant in many growth industries, these studies take on issues related to the consequences and costs of failure, especially in young and growing firms. Thus, the main sources for firm decline originate from various environmental, ecological, organizational, and psychological factors, all of which have been abundantly studied in the three research approaches. However, it is opportune to draw together their main findings and conclusions.

Deterministic perspective

In the deterministic perspective, explanations for firm failure are often sought from external sources. This is consistent with what has been argued about the dominant causes of industry decline identified in Chapter 2. Most environmental-ecological explanations of organizational decline indeed fall into the categories of customer behavior, innovation, market dynamics, industry maturity, legislation and policy, and exogenous events. However, some additional points have been made by population ecologists who have studied decline at the organizational level.

In the 1980s and 1990s, population ecology (Hannan and Freeman 1977, 1984) gained a strong foothold in strategy and management research; it was also applied in a large number of studies on firm failure. It formed (along with industrial organization economics) the first unified theoretical framework that was applied to the study of the birth, change, and mortality processes of organizational forms within diverse organizational populations (see Barron, West and Hannan 1994; Hannan and Freeman 1977, 1984). Here, the generic terms *population ecology* and *organizational ecology* are used interchangeably to refer to this 'deterministic' research tradition (Kücher and Feldbauer-Durstmüller 2019; Mellahi and Wilkinson 2004). Within this strand of research, organizations that are able to reproduce routines reliably and consistently (Nelson and Winter 1982), and improve their abilities continuously, ultimately create a competitive advantage and benefit from their reduced probability of failure (Heine and Rindfleisch 2013).

Population ecology is in sharp contrast with contemporary approaches that focus on managerial thinking and action leading to organizational adaptation (or the lack of it). It maintains that the success or failure of the firm is largely, if not totally, dependent on its own structural characteristics (e.g., product range, size, age) and how they match with the evolution of the business environment (e.g., the number of entries or exits to the target industry in question, or changes in customers' buying behavior). Young and small firms were often found to fail as they were short of the tangible and intangible resources to compete with larger, older, and more established incumbent corporations. Top management was perceived to be able to do nothing or very little to change this dynamic in the short run, leading to rapid organizational failures, followed by exits by bankruptcy or by merger and acquisition.

The results of population ecologists emphasized the importance of the right organizational form aligned to the evolutionary logic of the focal industry in explaining success or failure. Some firms were just lucky to be producing the goods or services and more customers became willing to buy at a given time period, and others failed since they were not able to launch successful offerings to that market segment in a timely manner. In the longer term, a company's reliability in reproducing effective and efficient routines to keep up with competition or to match the company's offerings with changing consumer tastes and needs kept the respective organizations alive and healthy. Thus, there was also some room for managerial maneuvering. However, it was maintained that too many and too great internal changes could also easily destroy the reliability of the corporation since change can "put established and inert organizations through the 'liabilities of newness' again" (Kücher and Feldbauer-Durstmüller 2019, p. 511).

In rapidly changing industries, increased failure rates for older firms were also detected, termed the "liabilities of aging" (Barron, West and Hannan 1994). Thus, the key findings from organizational ecology can explain the liabilities of both new and old firms. In contrast, Stinchcombe's (1965) widely referenced study assumed that new firms face disadvantages against incumbents ('liabilities of newness') in terms of entry barriers, problems in finding personnel, problems in building the organization and its connections to the environment, and worse financing conditions. This causes young firms to exhibit lower legitimacy because they have yet to create reliable routines to offer the requested stability. The length of different organizations' vulnerable "adolescence period" may be different and also depends on each organization's initial resources and capabilities (Kücher and Feldbauer-Durstmüller 2019, p. 10). Well-led and resourced young firms naturally thus tend to fare better than their less-endowed counterparts in one and the same industry setting. Organizational ecologists further claim that any organizational change hurts the reliability of organizations' performance and is thus detrimental to firm survival. In other words, change can force established organizations to face the liabilities of newness again and again. However, this can usually be managed if change does not happen too often (Amburgey, Kelly and Barnett 1993).

Population ecology scholars thus claim that the monotonic decline of failure probability by age does not exist if other conditions such as organization size and industry structure are controlled for. If industries indeed require change, one should also expect increased failure rates for incumbent firms. In other words, the "liabilities of aging" may also manifest (Barron, West and

Hannan 1994). The key findings from the deterministic approach thus provide explanations for the liabilities of both new and old firms. In this sense, organizational ecology provides a useful framework for studying dynamic organizational-level processes such as "downward spirals," which help explain paths both to and away from bankruptcy (Hambrick and D'Aveni 1988).

However, Mellahi and Wilkinson (2004, p. 27) argue that despite the important contribution of deterministic studies for understanding firm failure, they cannot explain why some firms survive while others fail under similar conditions. Several studies have also demonstrated that company performance is more strongly determined by the strategy adopted by the firm than industry conditions. By concentrating only on external factors to explain organizational failure, the authors believe that organizational ecology perspective is overly deterministic, and that only the most robust external effects can be detected by their methods. Consequently, the same authors continue that firm-internal factors that most often offer a more plausible explanation of organizational failure are grossly ignored in this paradigm, because they are too subtle to be measured adequately by the rather blunt research tools utilized by these researchers. As a consequence, there was a movement away from population ecology and toward firm-level research and a more voluntaristic (or managerial) approach and the strategic choice paradigm which dominated organizational decline and failure studies between 2001 and 2007 (Kücher and Feldbauer-Durstmüller 2019, p. 12).

Voluntaristic perspective

According to the voluntaristic perspective, firm managers' perceptions of the external environment have a strong effect on how they (mis)manage their firm. Consequently, managerial actions are influenced by the managers' mental models of the organization and its environment, and constrained, for instance, by their commitments, power and capacity to implement or enforce them (Mellahi and Wilkinson 2004, pp. 27–28). By the 1970s, Starbuck, Greve and Hedberg (1978) located the main source of organizational failure in the (mis)perceptions of organizational members, most importantly top executives. The main reasons for failure therefore often reside in the managers' minds. For instance, Macoby (2000) narrates how visionary managers can often be highly narcissistic and increase the risk of failure when business conditions abruptly change. Average top executives may also be highly inert in their thinking, unwilling to challenge their conventional business wisdom when external conditions change, either gradually or abruptly.

When it comes to the critiques of the voluntaristic paradigm, Mellahi and Wilkinson (2004, p. 31) point out to its strong reliance on several middle-range theories without an overarching grand theory as a major weakness.

Unlike organizational ecology, which has well-defined research aims and methodology (explaining firm survival and death through population-level quantitative modeling), scholars in the voluntaristic paradigm tend to deal with several, often uncoordinated and unrelated, company-internal issues in explaining firm demise. Thus, a common criticism of the voluntaristic perspective is its over-reliance on firm-internal factors, neglecting the context in which failing firms operate. Another problem is identified in the fact that virtually all such studies have been traditionally limited to only one country: the United States (Mellahi and Wilkinson 2004, p. 31).

Entrepreneurial perspective

Finally, according to the bibliometric review by Kücher and Feldbauer-Durstmüller (2019), after 2008 the dominant viewpoints of population ecology (external conditions explaining decline) and behavioral strategy (management psychology and action explaining decline) have been complemented – if not eclipsed – by an emerging entrepreneurial perspective. That is to say, the consequences of failure for those affected by company demise rather than the causes and reasons for failure have become the central object of study in the emerging entrepreneurial approach to firm decline (Ucbasaran et al. 2013). The main research areas of this research cluster focus on the financial, psychological, and social costs of failure, perceptions and attributions of failure, sense-making and learning in failure situations and processes, stigmatization and fear of failure as an attribute of organizational failures, and, finally, on entrepreneur-friendly (or entrepreneur-hostile) legal environments.

Consequently, this emerging research stream explores "how entrepreneurs perceive, make sense of, learn from, and respond to failure" (Ucbasaran et al. 2013, p. 164). According to Ucbasaran and colleagues (2013, p. 174), firm failure is always followed by an explicit or implicit assessment of the financial, social, and psychological costs of failure (and their interrelationships), and through the related social-psychological sensemaking and learning processes (at the individual and organizational levels), leading to the eventual outcomes of the entrepreneurial failure process, including personal recovery, and other cognitive and behavioral outcomes:

> In this sense, scholars referred to both the potential benefit through learning and sense-making and the emotional, social, and financial consequences of failure. Whereas scholars agreed that learning from failure is a benefit to those who learn, because learning increases experience, which in turn may foster firm performance, they also pointed out the difficulties that exist in learning from failure.
>
> (Kücher and Feldbauer-Durstmüller 2019, p. 512)

In what follows, we review the most important findings from the above-mentioned three paradigms from the viewpoint of the following questions: a) what happens during organizational decline; and b) how can organizational decline be managed?

What typically happens during organizational decline

Levinthal (1991) famously described organizational change and decline as a "random walk." Several organizations remain inactive and benefit from changed environmental conditions, whereas others try to adapt to changing industry conditions, potentially escaping the liabilities of aging. It is impossible to predict who will win and who will lose.

The management-oriented research stream began when Argenti (1976) investigated the managerial reasons for firm failure and the ensuing patterns of what he called "corporate collapse." According to Argenti (1976), a central reason for failure in mature companies was a "defective response to change," in other words, top managers' failure to respond effectively and efficiently to changes in their lines of business. Along these lines, the common denominator among strategic choice studies has been the focus on managerial thinking and action and their central role in explaining firm failure. Qualitative longitudinal case study designs have been common in this stream of research (Kücher and Feldbauer-Durstmüller 2019).

Time is arguably an important issue in most studies of strategic choice. As Buckley (2020) puts it in a recent account on the importance of historical research in international business studies:

> Macro time, at the level of the firm's environment, depends on long cycles of technology (creation, refinement, commercialization, standardization), product cycles (Vernon 1966) and market cycles (business cycles, fashion, secular trends, demography). Micro time, at the level of the firm, depends on the length of key contracts (Buckley, Craig and Mudambi 2019), on management decision making (team building, recruitment cycles), on investment and inventory decisions (including R&D).
>
> (p. 2)

All of these time-related issues can be found in strategic choice studies of firm failures, too. Untimely mismanagement of these issues thus often underpins firm decline and failure.

Most strategic choice studies have traditionally focused on the failure of large incumbent firms in established industries. In an early study in the voluntaristic genre, Hambrick and D'Aveni (1988) state that periods of organizational decline often last long; failure finally results from inadequate adaptation to new environmental needs due to organizational inertia, wrong managerial decisions and competitive actions, or sheer bad luck.

Strategic choice studies have also found that patterns of organizational decline tend to follow specific phases or stages: the failure of firm management to anticipate something in the business environment (blinded); the failure to take corrective action (inaction), wrong or inadequate decisions (faulty action); crisis; and finally firm dissolution (Weitzel and Jonsson 1989, p. 97). The length of these stages may vary greatly in an individual case, and each phase is characterized by its own managerial actions that drive decline toward the next phases (D'Aveni 1989; Weitzel and Jonsson 1989). Through turnaround and retrenchment attempts, managers may aim at deflecting the firm from its trajectory of failure, which naturally is not in any way preordained.

A significant proportion of research on organizational decline has investigated executive thought and (in)action as a central explanation for failures. However, in line with the well-known logic of the product life cycle and its famous phases of introduction, growth, maturity, and decline (Vernon 1966), the idea that the creation, transformation, and decline of business firms would follow the organizational life cycle (Kimberly and Miles 1980) had become widely accepted by the 1970s and the 1980s. Individual firms could naturally follow their idiosyncratic evolutionary paths, but in general, the organizational life-cycle argument was thought to hold in most (non-monopolistic) industries and (market economy) countries. Longitudinal studies on firm evolution were called for to prove the point. In single-product small firms, naturally, the product life cycle and the organizational life cycle would be almost identical. However, when a small firm grew to a multi-product firm and potentially later developed or acquired several business units with different business models, the organizational or corporate life cycle would deviate from the rather deterministic life cycle of traditional tangible products at the micro level of the corporation.

Organizational-psychological explanations of firm decline see change as more beneficial than detrimental and explain failures as failed processes of the firm to adapt to sudden environmental changes (D'Aveni 1989; Heine and Rindfleisch 2013; Staw, Sandelands and Dutton 1981; Weitzel and Jonsson 1989). These studies have tended to focus on what went wrong in adaptation processes (Hambrick and D'Aveni 1988), what attributes are often found in declining firms in general (Cameron, Kim and Whetten 1987), what factors caused organizational failure, and why some firms survive organizational decline while others do not (D'Aveni 1989; Weitzel and Jonsson 1989).

Failure may also be seen as a turnaround that did not work; top management was not able to retrench the organization and exit the path of failure (Sheppard and Chowdhury 2005). A large literature has thus emerged especially on organizational turnarounds, which were naturally assumed to be preceded by a period of identifiable decline (see, e.g., Trahms, Ndofor and Sirmon 2013). Many studies have focused on the antecedents, processes, and outcomes of decline and consequent turnaround attempts (e.g., Barker and Barr 2002). Both quantitative and qualitative research designs have been employed, but the approach has been innately managerial: what should the top management of a declining firm do in a turnaround attempt? Since timing is critical in a declining firm, how should different actions be prioritized and how should their implementation be timed?

If a company's short-term managerial focus is on *exploitation*, in the middle or long term, however, the organization must also guarantee that its offerings remain competitive and focus on *exploration* in terms on R&D, other innovation activities and product development. Many firms enter declining developmental paths in one or both activity groups as "threat rigidity processes" impede a successful turnaround because management tends to focus on short-term goals at the expense of strategic change, large-scale adaptation processes, or longer-term innovation (D'Aveni 1989; Staw, Sandelands and Dutton 1981).

According to the seminal study by Cameron, Kim and Whetten (1987), declining organizations are characterized by increased secrecy, rigidity, high personnel turnover, formalization, and centralization, whereas their innovativeness, long-term planning, leader influence, and employee morale tend to decrease. On the basis of literature, Mellahi and Wilkinson (2004, p. 31) identify five psychological factors (denial, rationalization, idealization, fantasy, and symbolization) that have been discussed as barriers to individual and organizational learning, but they are also relevant to organizational failures.

Through *denial*, managers seek to disclaim knowledge and responsibility and to disavow acts and their consequences (Brown and Starkey 2000). Therefore, top management denial can have profound implications for organizational failure. For instance, Mellahi, Jackson and Spark (2002) described how the retail chain Marks and Spencer's top management's rejection of customer feedback surveys blinded them and led them to deny that there was a problem until the company faced a full-blown crisis.

Rationalization is an attempt to justify the impulses, needs, feelings, actions, and motives that one finds unacceptable so that they become both plausible and consciously tolerable (Brown and Starkey 2000). Organizational failure often involves a lot of rationalization of bad practices and a defunct organizational culture.

Idealization is a process by which some object comes to be overvalued and stripped of any negative features. Idealization processes thus help explain why managers often escalate their commitment to a failing strategy or a course of action as they undergo the risk of additional negative outcomes to justify prior behavior (cf. "commitment escalation" in Staw 1976).

Fantasy is an unconscious endeavor to meet difficult or impossible goals and aspirations. In organizations, fantasies are forms of collective retreat into imagination, often destructive to the organization.

Finally, *symbolization* is the process "through which an external object becomes the disguised outward representation for another internal and hidden object, idea, person, or complex" (Laughlin 1970, p. 414). In other words, managers use symbols to manipulate and control their organizations (Brown and Starkey 2000).

Since 2000, many studies have looked at firm decline processes from the viewpoint of organizational learning (Kücher and Feldbauer-Durstmüller 2019). The starting point was that firm failure can be seen as a consequence of not being able to adjust the routines of the organization to meet the changing demands of the business environment (especially in terms of changing customer needs and changes in competition). A failure to balance corporate exploration and exploitation when new products are needed in key target markets is a case in point. In several cases, organizational learning failure could be diagnosed as the main reason for firm decline.

In addition, narrative research approaches to organizational decline and turnaround have also emerged in the 2000s, positing that narratives and representations of decline and turnaround could be analyzed with variegated theoretical frameworks adapted from literary theory (Lamberg and Pajunen 2005). However, it is beyond the scope of this chapter to review the extensive literature on retrenchment and turnarounds per se. Our focus here is on the decline process of the organization as a unit of analysis in unpacking reasons and outcomes for firm failure.

How organizational decline can be managed

According to the voluntaristic paradigm, in the short term, the operating routines of the firm need to be continuously improved in order to guarantee efficiency and effectiveness in competitive conditions often resembling Red Queen competition in most contemporary industries (a situation in which everyone tries harder but there are no competitive gains to anyone since everybody is running faster on average than earlier). The short-term focus is thus on *exploitation*, not *exploration*. Two main perspectives to organizational learning can be identified in this respect (Kücher and Feldbauer-Durstmüller 2019). First, the need to frequently change the firm and its business model(s) in the changing business environment requires constant adaptations and the top management and the firm need to learn "how to change." The organization thus needs to learn how to quickly change its operating routines, and consequent "modification routines" can be distinguished (Amburgey, Kelly and Barnett 1993; Nelson and Winter 1982).

The second perspective answers the question of whether and how firms can learn from failure. Firms have traditionally been assumed to learn mainly from success, but increased routinization and an overconfidence in successful adaptations in the past may lead to firm failure in the future (Sitkin 1992). In the middle or long term, an organization must guarantee that its offerings remain competitive and focus on exploration in terms on savvy R&D, other innovation activities and successful product development and market launch activity (D'Aveni 1989; Staw, Sandelands and Dutton 1981).

The failure of the leading global cellular-phone manufacturer Nokia in 2007–2008 is a case in point. Lamberg et al. (2021) investigated how and why the Nokia Corporation failed to develop a successful strategic response to the threats of Apple and Google in the smartphone business and instead worsened its situation through several badly timed decisions. The authors identified key choices in technology and organizational design that jointly constituted sufficient cause for the abandonment of the mobile phone business, sold to Microsoft in 2013. The incapacity to rapidly learn from own failures, for instance, in launching successive smartphone generations was a central factor in explaining Nokia's demise. In general, companies that try to learn from their failures or even use small-scale failures as lessons in how to operate better in the future may be more efficient in their organizational learning than those firms that try to learn only from their past successes.

Furthermore, several studies have emphasized that successful companies seem capable of learning from their failures or, even to use small failures to learn to be able to do better in future bigger cases such as product launches (e.g., Baumard and Starbuck 2005; Sitkin 1992). However, learning from failure is especially difficult at the individual, group, and organizational levels due to numerous psychological (e.g., excessive self-confidence of key actors) and group-related (e.g., stigmatization of those who have failed) barriers to learning (Cannon and Edmondson 2001).

Zacharakis, Meyer and DeCastro (1999) see attribution bias among entrepreneurs when evaluating their own and others' failures. The failures of others were attributed to manageable factors to a higher degree – own failures were attributed to external, unmanageable factors. This is hardly surprising. Significant attribution differences also occur between entrepreneurs and other stakeholders, especially venture capitalists. Attribution bias may hinder drawing the right conclusions and result in inefficient resource allocation or bad investment decisions in future business activities (Ucbasaran et al. 2013). Reflecting on potential attribution bias is thus an important managerial implication on how to approach firm failure *ex post*. Why did a certain start-up, for example, fail? What were the key antecedents and processes that led to failure? Do different stakeholders identify different issues as important at different levels of analysis?

The media data of Cardon, Stevens and Potter (2011) on small firm failures indicated that blaming the entrepreneurs and their mistakes occurred as often as pointing to external factors and chance emanating from the environment. Contextual differences in different regions and countries are marked. In addition to the influence of perceived stigma at the societal level, there have been several influential studies on stigmatization at the organizational and individual levels (Sutton and Callahan 1987; Wiesenfeld, Wurthmann and Hambrick 2008). Consequently, in the entrepreneurial approach to firm failure, research focus has often been on institutions that hinder the success of entrepreneurial firms. For instance, the potential of developing entrepreneur-friendly law systems has recently received increased attention (Fan and White 2003; Peng, Yamakawa and Lee 2010).

Another central institution whose lacking development might cause entrepreneurial firms to fail are clusters and ecosystems of other firms and supporting organizations. Generally, clusters and ecosystems of other firms and supporting organizations are central institutions whose lacking development might cause entrepreneurial failures. Thus, entrepreneurship itself is an important institution – for instance, the level of entrepreneurial activity, a major source of economic development and growth in any country, is directly related to the stigmatization of failures and optimal bankruptcy systems should make a "fresh start" (Ayotte 2007) or a "second chance" (European Commission 2011) possible, which would foster entrepreneurship at a societal level.

Summary

This chapter provided an overview of research on organizational decline and how decline can be managed. We have focused on four areas: what constitutes decline, what causes decline, what happens during decline, and how decline can be managed. In each section, we have highlighted how the deterministic, voluntaristic, and entrepreneurial perspectives have answered these questions.

To answer *what constitutes decline*, we have highlighted how organizational failure is the most frequently used concept to depict organizational decline and it can occur due to company internal reasons, external reasons, or a combination. The common symptoms of organizational decline include shrinking financial resources, negative profitability, shrinking market, loss of legitimacy, exit from international markets, and severe erosion of market share.

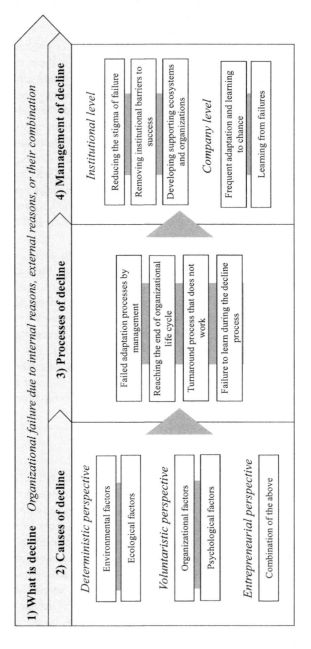

Figure 4.3 Integrative framework of organizational decline research

To understand *what causes decline*, research provides us with four determinants:

1 Environmental factors (including technological change, regulatory factors, demographic and economic change)
2 Ecological factors pertaining to the industry and the company (including age, size, density, industry life cycle)
3 Organizational factors (including top management composition and tenure, homogeneity, succession, past performance)
4 Psychological factors (focusing on managerial (mis)perceptions and cognitions)

While analyzing these four causes for decline, we introduced the three central perspectives: deterministic, voluntaristic, and entrepreneurial.

Thereafter, we examined *what happens during organizational decline*, which led us to uncover several processes that explain organizational decline. The four central processes involved in organizational decline are:

1 Failed adaptation processes by management
2 Reaching the end of organizational life cycle (which is similar to the end of product or industry life cycle)
3 Decline as a turnaround process that did not work (management was unable to retrench the organization)
4 Failure to learn during the decline process (due to psychological reasons including denial, rationalization, idealization, fantasy, and symbolization)

Finally, we outlined *how organizational decline can be managed*. On the institutional level, we highlighted that decline and its consequences can be mitigated by reducing the stigma of failure, by removing institutional barriers to success and by developing supporting ecosystems and organizations. On the company level, the two pertinent remedies for the management of decline are:

1 Frequent adaptation and learning to change (to minimize the chances of decline)
2 Learning from failures (large or small)

These analyses enable the reader to understand how organizational decline has been analyzed from the three key perspectives and what each perspective can teach us about the causes, processes, and management of decline. These takeaways are summarized in Figure 4.3.

Suggestions for further reading

To become better acquainted with organizational decline, we recommend three academic works. Two of these studies are journal articles that provide complementary overviews of the literature, and the third is a book that focuses on organizational decline:

- Heine, K., & Rindfleisch, H. (2013). Organizational decline: A synthesis of insights from organizational ecology, path dependence and the resource-based view. *Journal of Organizational Change Management, 26*(1), 8–28. DOI: 10.1108/09534811311307888
- Kücher, A., & Feldbauer-Durstmüller, B. (2019) Organizational failure and decline – A bibliometric study of the scientific frontend. *Journal of Business Research,* 98, 503–516. DOI: 10.1016/j.jbusres.2018.05.017
- Cameron, K. S., Sutton, R. I., & Whetten, D. A. (1988). *Readings in Organizational Decline: Frameworks, Research, and Prescriptions.* Cambridge: Ballinger.

References

Amburgey, T. L., Kelly, D., & Barnett, W. P. (1993). Resetting the clock: The dynamics of organizational change and failure. *Administrative Science Quarterly, 38*(1), 51–73. https://doi.org/10.2307/2393254

Argenti, J. (1976). *Corporate Collapse – The Causes and Symptoms.* New York: Halstead Press.

Ayotte, K. (2007). Bankruptcy and entrepreneurship: The value of a fresh start. *Journal of Law, Economics, and Organization, 23*(1), 161–185. https://doi.org/10.1093/jleo/ewm007

Barker, V. L., & Barr, P. S. (2002). Linking top manager attributions to strategic reorientation in declining firms attempting turnarounds. *Journal of Business Research, 55*(12), 963–979. https://doi.org/10.1016/S0148-2963(00)00217-4

Barron, D. N., West, E., & Hannan, T. M. (1994). A time to grow and a time to die: Growth and mortality of credit unions in New York City, 1914–1990. *American Journal of Sociology, 100*(2), 381–421. https://doi.org/10.1086/230541

Baumard, P., & Starbuck, W. H. (2005). Learning from failures: Why it may not happen. *Long Range Planning, 38*(3), 281–298. https://doi.org/10.1016/j.lrp.2005.03.004

Benson, J. (1975). Interorganizational networks as a political economy. *Administrative Science Quarterly, 20*(2), 229–249. https://doi.org/10.2307/2391696

Brown, A. D., & Starkey, K. (2000). Organizational identity and organizational learning: A psychodynamic perspective. *Academy of Management Review, 25*(1), 102–120. https://doi.org/10.5465/amr.2000.2791605

Buckley, P. J (2020). The role of history in international business: Evidence, research practices, methods and theory. *British Journal of Management,* forthcoming, https://doi.org/10.1111/1467-8551.12446

Buckley, P. J., Craig, T. D., & Mudambi, R. (2019). Time to learn? Assignment duration in global value chain organization. *Journal of Business Research, 103*, 547–556. https://doi.org/10.1016/j.jbusres.2018.01.011

Burt, S. L., Mellahi, K., Jackson, P., & Sparks, L. (2002). Retail internationalization and retail failure: Issues from the case of Marks and Spencer. *International Review of Retail, Distribution and Consumer Research, 12*(2), 191–219. https://doi.org/10.1080/09593960210127727

Busenbark, J. R., Krause, R., Boivie, S., & Graffin, S. D. (2016). Toward a configurational perspective on the CEO: A review and synthesis of the management literature. *Journal of Management, 42*(1), 234–268. https://doi.org/10.1177/0149206315618448

Cameron, K. S. (1983). Strategic responses to conditions of decline: Higher education and the private sector. *Journal of Higher Education, 54*, 359–380.

Cameron, K. S., Kim, M. U., & Whetten, D. A. (1987). Organizational effects of decline and turbulence. *Administrative Science Quarterly, 32*(4), 222–240. https://doi.org/0.1080/00221546.1983.11778210

Cameron, K. S., Sutton, R. I., & Whetten, D. A. (1988). *Readings in Organizational Decline: Frameworks, Research, and Prescriptions*. Cambridge: Ballinger.

Cannon, M. D., & Edmondson, A. C. (2001). Confronting failure: Antecedents and consequences of shared beliefs about failure in organizational work groups. *Journal of Organizational Behavior, 22*(2), 161–177. https://doi.org/10.1002/job.85

Cardon, M. S., Stevens, C. E., & Potter, D. R. (2011). Misfortunes or mistakes? Cultural sensemaking of entrepreneurial failure. *Journal of Business Venturing, 26*(1), 79–92. https://doi.org/10.1016/j.jbusvent.2009.06.004

D'Aveni, R. A. (1989). The aftermath of organizational decline: A longitudinal study of the strategic and managerial characteristics of declining firms. *Academy of Management Journal, 32*(3), 577–605. https://doi.org/10.5465/256435

European Commission. (2011). *A Second Chance for Entrepreneurs: Prevention of Bankruptcy, Simplification of Bankruptcy Procedures and Support for a Fresh Start*. Bruxelles: Enterprise and Industry Directorate-General. Retrieved from http://ec.europa.eu/DocsRoom/documents/10451/attachments/1/translations/en/renditions/n (21.12.2020).

Fan, W., & White, M. J. (2003). Personal bankruptcy and the level of entrepreneurial activity. *Journal of Law and Economics, 46*(2), 543–567. https://doi.org/10.1086/382602

Hambrick, D. C., & D'Aveni, R. A. (1988). Large corporate failures as downward spirals. *Administrative Science Quarterly, 33*(1), 1–23. https://doi.org/10.2307/2392853

Hannan, M. T., & Freeman, J. H. (1977). The population ecology of organizations. *American Journal of Sociology, 82*(5), 929–964. https://doi.org/10.1086/226424

Hannan, M. T., & Freeman, J. H. (1984). Structural inertia and organizational change. *American Sociological Review, 49*(2), 149–164. https://doi.org/10.2307/2095567

Harrigan, K. R. (1982). Exit decisions in mature industries. *Academy of Management Journal, 25*(4), 707–732. https://doi.org/10.5465/256095

Heine, K., & Rindfleisch, H. (2013). Organizational decline: A synthesis of insights from organizational ecology, path dependence and the resource-based view. *Journal of Organizational Change Management, 26*(1), 8–28. https://doi.org/10.1108/09534811311307888

Jackson, P., Mellahi, K., & Sparks, L. (2005). Shutting up shop: Understanding the international exit process in retailing. *The Service Industries Journal, 25*(3), 355–371. https://doi.org/10.1080/02642060500050475

Kimberly, J. R., & Miles, R. H. (Eds.). (1980). *The Organizational Life Cycle: Issues in the Creation, Transformation and Decline of Organizations.* San Francisco: Jossey-Bass Inc.

Kücher, A., & Feldbauer-Durstmüller, B. (2019). Organizational failure and decline – A bibliometric study of the scientific frontend. *Journal of Business Research, 98*, 503–516. https://doi.org/10.1016/j.jbusres.2018.05.017

Lamberg, J.-A., Lubinaitė, S., Ojala, J., & Tikkanen, H. (2021). The curse of agility: The Nokia Corporation and the loss of market dominance in mobile phones, 2003–2013. *Business History, 63*(4), 574–605. https://doi.org/10.1080/00076791.2019.1593964

Lamberg, J.-A., & Pajunen, K. (2005). Beyond the metaphor: The morphology of organizational decline and turnaround. *Human Relations, 58*(8), 947–980. https://doi.org/10.1177/0018726705058499

Laughlin, H. P. (1970). *The Ego and Its Defenses.* New York: Appleton-Century-Crofts.

Levinthal, D. (1991). Random walks and organizational mortality. *Administrative Science Quarterly, 36*(3), 397–420. https://doi.org/10.2307/2393202

Macoby, M. (2000). Narcissistic leaders: The incredible pros, the inevitable cons. *Harvard Business Review, 78*(1), 68–78.

Mellahi, K., Jackson, P., & Sparks, L. (2002). An exploratory study into failure in successful organizations: The case of Marks and Spencer. *British Journal of Management, 13*(1), 15–30. https://doi.org/10.1111/1467-8551.00220

Mellahi, K., & Wilkinson, A. (2004). Organizational failure: A critique of recent research and a proposed integrative framework. *International Journal of Management Reviews, 5–6*(1), 21–41. https://doi.org/10.1111/j.1460-8545.2004.00095.x

Mellahi, K., & Wilkinson, A. (2010). Managing and coping with organizational failure: Introduction to the special issue. *Group & Organization Management, 35*(5), 531–541. https://doi.org/10.1177/1059601110383404

Miller, D. (1981). Toward a new contingency approach: The search for organizational gestalts. *Journal of Management Studies, 18*(1), 1–26. https://doi.org/10.1111/j.1467-6486.1981.tb00088.x

Mintzberg, H. (1979). *The Structuring of Organizations.* Prentice Hall: Englewood Cliffs.

Nelson, R. R., & Winter, S. G. (1982). *An Evolutionary Theory of Economic Change.* Cambridge, MA: Harvard University Press.

Peng, M. W., Yamakawa, Y., & Lee, S. H. (2010). Bankruptcy laws and entrepreneur-friendliness. *Entrepreneurship Theory and Practice, 34*(3), 517–530. https://doi.org/10.1111/j.1540-6520.2009.00350.x

Sheppard, J. P., & Chowdhury, S. D. (2005). Riding the wrong wave: Organizational failure as a failed turnaround. *Long Range Planning, 38*(3), 239–260. https://doi.org/10.1016/j.lrp.2005.03.009

Sitkin, S. B. (1992). Learning through failure: The strategy of small losses. *Research in Organizational Behavior, 14*, 231–266.

Smith, W. K., Binns, A., & Tushman, M. L. (2010). Complex business models: Managing strategic paradoxes simultaneously. *Long Range Planning, 43*(2–3), 448–461. https://doi.org/10.1016/j.lrp.2009.12.003

Starbuck, W. H., Greve, A., & Hedberg, B. L. T. (1978). Responding to crisis. *Journal of Business Administration, 9*(2), 111–137.

Staw, B. M. (1976). Knee-deep in the big muddy: A study of escalating commitment to a course of action. *Organizational Behavior and Human Performance, 16*(1), 27–44. https://doi.org/10.1016/0030-5073(76)90005-2

Staw, B. M., Sandelands, L. E., & Dutton, J. E. (1981). Threat-rigidity effects in organizational behavior: A multilevel analysis. *Administrative Science Quarterly, 26*(4), 501–524. https://doi.org/10.2307/2392337

Stinchcombe, A. L. (1965). Social structure and organizations. In J. G. March (Ed.), *The Handbook of Organizations* (pp. 142–193). Chicago: Rand McNally & Co.

Sutton, R. I., & Callahan, A. L. (1987). The stigma of bankruptcy: Spoiled organizational image and its management. *Academy of Management Journal, 30*(3), 405–436. https://doi.org/10.5465/256007

Trahms, C. A., Ndofor, H. A., & Sirmon, D. G. (2013). Organizational decline and turnaround: A review and agenda for future research. *Journal of Management, 39*(5), 1277–1307. https://doi.org/10.1177/0149206312471390

Ucbasaran, D., Shepherd, D. A., Lockett, A., & Lyon, S. J. (2013). Life after business failure: The process and consequences of business failure for entrepreneurs. *Journal of Management, 39*(1), 163–202. https://doi.org/10.1177/0149206312457823

Vernon, R. (1966). International investment and international trade in the product cycle. *Quarterly Journal of Economics, 80*(2), 190–207. https://doi.org/10.2307/1880689

Weitzel, W., & Jonsson, E. (1989). Decline in organizations: A literature integration and extension. *Administrative Science Quarterly, 34*(1), 91–109. https://doi.org/10.2307/2392987

Wiesenfeld, B. M., Wurthmann, K. A., & Hambrick, D. C. (2008). The stigmatization and devaluation of elites associated with corporate failures: A process model. *Academy of Management Review, 33*(1), 231–251. https://doi.org/10.5465/amr.2008.27752771

Zacharakis, A., Meyer, G., & DeCastro, J. (1999). Differing perceptions of new venture failure: A matched exploratory study of venture capitalists and entrepreneurs. *Journal of Small Business Management, 37*(3), 1–14.

5 Decline and its management across different levels of analysis

Themes and observations regarding decline as a phenomenon

In reviewing the literature on decline, several observations and themes emerged that we wish to emphasize. Not only do they illuminate shared intellectual foundations and themes that cut across different levels of analysis, but they also highlight how the levels of analysis relate to each other. These themes relate to the nature of decline, causes of decline, relationship between levels of analysis, and the outcomes of decline.

Forms and pace of decline

In the introductory chapter, we offered some definitions of *decline*. The definitions converge around the ideas that decline refers to something becoming worse, losing value, or becoming less important. This logic is present in the literature on the decline of industries, clusters, and organizations. What cuts across all of these levels is that decline can take three forms: 1) deterioration of the entity; 2) deterioration of the entity's relation to the environment; and 3) deterioration of the entity's capacity for renewal.

Deterioration of the studied entity is an obvious way to detect its decline. At the industry and cluster levels, this can be observed in falling production capacity, a decrease in the number of companies, and a drop in the number of employees (e.g., Donnelly, Begley and Collis 2017; Menzel and Fornahl 2010). A reduction in these factors reduces the pool of resources that an industry or a cluster has at its disposal. Similarly, the literature on organizational decline also maintains that decline can be observed from the reduction of resources that an organization commands (Cameron, Sutton and Whetten 1988). Therefore, the depletion of resources that an entity is able to muster characterizes its decline.

DOI: 10.4324/9781003035947-5

A business organization's deteriorating relationship with the environment is usually manifested in declining sales, market share, or demand for its offerings (e.g., Chandler, Broberg and Allison 2014; Harrigan and Porter 1983). These factors indicate that an industry, a cluster, or a company is unable to meet customer needs or to do so in a way that is superior to its direct or indirect competitors. This affects the resource pool that can be used to sustain activities for the long term.

The incapacity to renew oneself is another key form of decline. This is usually manifested in reduced capacity to adjust to environmental changes, reduced level of innovation, or reduced variation (in different kinds of companies and strategies) that would enable adaptation (e.g., Arora, Branstetter and Drev 2013; Cameron, Sutton and Whetten 1988; Menzel and Fornahl 2010). Deterioration of these factors creates a competitive disadvantage or mismatch with the environment that inevitably leads to the decline of the entity.

These three forms of decline interact and co-constitute decline across each other and the levels of analysis. This is because available resources, relationship with the environment, and capacity for renewal influence each other, and a change in any of these dimensions influence the other two. As an example of this co-evolutionary relationship, organizational failure is constituted by an organization's deteriorating adaptability and the accompanying reduction of resources (Cameron, Sutton and Whetten 1988). This implies a close relationship among the different forms of decline and how they co-constitute the decline process.

In addition to the different forms of decline, *the pace of decline* is an important factor that characterizes different manifestations of decline. The distinction between continuous and discontinuous decline classically outlined by Zammuto and Cameron (1982) is helpful in this regard. On the one hand, continuous decline constitutes relatively predictable change over longer periods of time, where decline might not present itself as an immediate threat but rather as something that a company needs to adapt to and manage. Discontinuous change, on the other hand, is primarily characterized by rapid and unexpected changes that can cause tumult and lead to potential collapse even in the short term. This is immediate cause for concern as decline becomes unpredictable and felt by the involved actors.

With increasing globalization and the onslaught of events that can rapidly create decline (such as the September 11, 2001, terrorist attacks, the global financial crisis, the Eurozone crisis, and the Covid-19 crisis), we can speculate whether these kinds of abrupt changes pose the greatest challenge for businesses since they seem to occur more frequently than earlier and tend to come unannounced. In this regard, academia has also followed suit with publications such as the 2020 "Doomsday Scenarios" special issue in

Academy of Management Perspectives. However, there is still much to be done to increase our understanding of discontinuous decline and the rapid collapse it can cause to industries, clusters, and firms.

Technological change

Technological change can be identified as a key factor that causes decline across all levels of analysis. In doing so, it is usually perceived as an external change that one needs to adapt to. On the one hand, technological change can directly cause decline when technologies that industries, clusters, or companies rely upon are displaced by more efficient and advanced technologies. This directly leads to a disadvantageous situation that precipitates decline. For instance, Lamberg and colleagues (2021) attribute Nokia's decline partly to the company's reliance on the Symbian operating system that became outdated when competition shifted toward smartphones and platforms.

On the other hand, technological change can cause a slower decline if there are structural impediments to adaptation. For instance, the highly influential studies on the British cotton industry by Lazonick (1981, 1983) depict how the industry declined because of an ingrained mindset on how the industry should operate, which impeded the adoption of new innovations. So, while technological change can be seen as a motor for progress and development, it is a Janus-faced phenomenon that often causes decline in its wake.

Resources and capabilities

Challenges related to resources and capabilities are another key cause for decline that spans different levels of analysis. Resources and capabilities cover the productive inputs and the tools and technologies that are used to manufacture final products, and the financial and human resource assets that are used to sustain those activities. Decline is usually caused by changes in the *level* and *type* of resources and capabilities.

What we call a *level* is often associated with the depletion of resources that causes decline or it is associated with fewer resources and capabilities than what competitors have. In this way, depletion of natural resources is an obvious cause for the decline of industries and clusters, while lower level of resources can put young and small firms at a disadvantage relative to their larger counterparts that have a wider resource base at their disposal.

It is also possible that an industry, a cluster, or a company ends up having inferior *types* of resources or capabilities in order to stay competitive. This is often the case when the core capabilities of a company become rigidities

(Leonard-Barton 1992) or when industries and clusters mature and focus too much on their past activities which limits the diversity of resources and capabilities. This interferes with the capability to renew oneself and match changes in the business environment.

Interconnected life cycles across levels of analysis

Life cycles are a key explanatory model that keeps appearing in this book. While the idea originates from Vernon's (1966) seminal product life-cycle concept, it has since been applied to industries (Klepper 1997), clusters (Menzel and Fornahl 2010), and individual organizations (Kimberly and Miles 1980), too. The widespread use of life-cycle logic has two important ramifications.

In explaining decline, the life-cycle model provides a universal description of the development trajectory that inevitably leads to decline and eventually to death. The characteristics of this final stage before expiration include specialization, concentration, decrease in demand, and lacking diversity. For instance, at the industry level this means that during decline an industry concentrates on a few specialized companies while others exit the business entirely (Karniouchina et al. 2013). Thus, life-cycle logic is highly suitable for mapping out development trajectories and characterizing what decline is like across levels of analysis.

In addition, life cycles are interconnected across levels of analysis. A simple example of this interconnected logic is the decline of a dominant single product company where the product, organization, cluster, and industry life cycles could converge to explain the demise of this single entity (and, at the same time, the cluster and industry it once so strongly dominated). While this example is obviously an overstatement, the interconnected logic of life cycles is visible in the preceding chapters. For instance, Dalum, Pedersen and Villumsen (2005) recount how the life cycle of the NorCOM wireless communication cluster in the North Jutland was tied to the life cycles of different mobile phone technologies. Thus, accounting for the interconnected nature life cycles across levels can deepen our understanding of how and why different levels of analysis relate to each other. Simultaneously, understanding life cycles across levels allows managers to understand the state of their offerings, the state of the company itself, and the state of the industry or cluster in which it operates.

Multilevel dynamics

To this point in this book, we have analyzed decline by limiting our focus to a single level of analysis, whether that is the industry, a cluster, or a company. However, this distinction is always a matter of definition and is in the eye of the beholder. For instance, several studies discuss the decline of the big US automakers in Detroit by defining them as an industry (Freedman and Blair 2010) or a cluster (Hannigan, Cano-Kollmann and Mudambi 2015). However, one could also argue that the Detroit automakers should be analyzed as individual companies due to their diverging business strategies and resulting idiosyncratic nature.

While the challenge of making these distinctions might look like laxity in defining the unit of analysis, we argue that it reveals the interconnectedness between levels of analysis. Inherently, industries are made up of individual companies and clusters span multiple industries. Similarly, individual companies can participate in multiple industries by offering different goods and relocate in order to become part of clusters that enable them to take advantage of agglomeration economies in several business settings. There are already studies that span levels of analysis and shed light on these multilevel dynamics (e.g., Dalum, Pedersen and Villumsen 2005; Donnelly, Begley and Collis 2017; Lamberg et al. 2021).

Analyzing these multilevel dynamics foregrounds the importance of *nanoeconomics:* the analysis of clusters and industries through the individual companies that they are made of (see Klepper 2016 for origins and closer description of this approach). In this regard, the recent study by Lamberg and Peltoniemi (2020) bridges firm-level decision-making and industry evolution to analyze the evolution of the global pulp and paper industry. In this connection, Braguinsky and Hounshell's (2016) study of Japan's cotton spinning industry demonstrates the value of combining nanoeconomics and historical methods in studying the co-evolution of firms and an industry. It is our contention that these kinds of nanoeconomic analyses could provide further insights on the multilevel dynamics that pertain to decline in general. Especially, the investigation of firm-level strategic choices and subsequent strategic developments open up entirely new perspectives into the industry- and cluster-level evolution – not only more nuanced but also theoretically innovative.

Extinction, collapse, and death

The endpoint of decline is extinction, collapse, or death. Interestingly though, the literature on industries and clusters often frames decline as a possibility for renewal and change or as a slow process that settles in over time. Therefore, decline rarely has a definitive endpoint where an industry, cluster, and the associated companies would simply cease to exist. As examples, Kuilman and van Driel (2013) analyzed how a specific category of warehousing companies in Rotterdam disappeared as its members started to deviate from the characteristics of that category and became part of another, while De Propris and Lazzeretti (2009) analyzed how the Birmingham Jewelry Quarter slowly declined in the face of intensifying foreign competition. Thus, analyses on the decline of industries and clusters rarely reach the logical endpoint, which might be because companies migrate to new business areas and some remnants of the old are always left behind. As a contrast to this tendency, the literature on organizational decline and failure is much more aligned with the idea of an end, maybe because the liquidation or a bankruptcy of a company is an unmistakable endpoint. This might explain why this literature has examined the costs, learnings, and recovery processes that are associated with failure after it has happened.

Decline and renewal

While decline in and of itself can be depressing, it is not always the end. Many companies, clusters and industries continue to exist even after they undergo significant periods of decline. Decline can even have benefits since long-standing decline can deter companies from entering an industry that benefits the companies that have been able to survive.

Decline can also lead to renewal as dwindling companies, clusters, and industries find new growth trajectories that lead them out of decline. This can happen through the discovery of new technologies, markets, and functions for the organizations that act as the key to finding a path of recovery. For instance, the Detroit auto cluster (Hannigan, Cano-Kollmann and Mudambi 2015) and the Akron tire cluster (Mudambi, Mudambi, Mukherjee and Scalera 2017) transformed from declining production clusters into creators of new knowledge and technologies. This strategic change in the primary function was the key to the transformation and revitalization of these clusters. Similarly, focusing on new target markets has been a central prerequisite for the survival of many declining industries as new markets offset the impact that novel offerings by international competition have had in the home market (Adner and Snow 2010; Kalafsky and MacPherson 2002). Decline and renewal could therefore be conceived to occur in waves as companies seek new ways to utilize their resources when they face decline. This dynamic also drives change and renewal. Finally, this analysis of decline and renewal nicely segues into the second part of this chapter that explains how decline can be managed and how a new trajectory of growth can be found.

Management of decline

When analyzing how literature has treated the management of decline across industry, cluster, and company levels, we can identify four approaches: 1) preventing decline; 2) building a bridge to renewal; 3) structural change and renewal; and 4) letting go. In doing so, the potential actions for managing decline range from preventive measures that counter decline in the first place to structural changes when decline takes place and end with "letting go" at the point of no return. Figure 5.1 illustrates how the managerial implications presented in each chapter fall into these four categories.

Preventing decline

A substantial portion of literature highlights the need to prevent decline. In this literature, decline presumably emerges from the combination of two factors. It is assumed that competition, technologies, and customer needs change over time, which inevitably alters the business landscape, causing some actors to decline. In addition, industries, clusters, and companies become more focused over time, which reduces their diversity and capacity to adapt. Therefore, an industry, a cluster, or a company loses its competitiveness at some point in time because it becomes less efficient than its competitor or it simply produces goods that customers do not want. This is also consistent with the idea that a deteriorating relationship with the environment and incapacity to renew oneself were identified as two central forms of decline.

To prevent decline, it is necessary either to increase variation in the types of companies or activities that are carried out so that some of them might match with the changing environmental conditions or to improve an entity's capacity to adapt and renew itself to accommodate changing conditions. In practice, this can mean increasing competitive variety within an industry, investing into cluster-level innovation processes, or frequent adaptation and learning to change on the level of individual companies. A good example of the importance of variety and adaptation is provided by the industry decline literature which highlights that competitive variety can help protect industries against external threats (Miles, Snow and Sharfman 1993), while high level of innovation makes industries more adaptable to changing conditions (Arora, Branstetter and Drev 2013).

Building a bridge toward renewal

The second way of managing decline is building a bridge to renewal when decline happens. This approach consists of activities that don't necessarily generate structural changes but rather point to a potential path of recovery. These activities come in two forms: 1) provision of external support and 2) changing activities.

It is common that industries, clusters, and companies are provided with direct external support when they face decline. Recent examples include the

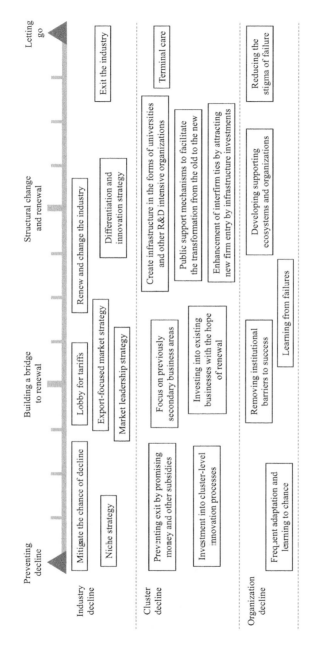

Figure 5.1 Management of decline across levels of analysis

US government bailout of General Motors and Chrysler during the financial crisis that began in 2007, the introduction of import tariffs on steel and aluminum by US President Trump, and introduction of the EU's Covid-19 recovery package that was intended to set Europe into a new growth trajectory through investments in digitalization and innovation. The academic literature has also highlighted the importance of similar actions such as using tariffs to shield industries from foreign competition, investing in existing businesses with the hope of renewal, or removing institutional barriers to the success of individual companies. In this regard, it seems that any industry, cluster, or company can be saved if there is the political will to do so.

Industries, clusters, and companies can also enter a new growth trajectory by changing how they function. In practice, this can mean finding new markets by focusing on previously secondary business areas or export markets. Another option is to aim for market leadership by increasing efficiency and market power that helps to fend off competition. Finally, smaller failures can also serve as a way to learn and adapt activities that cushion against serious blunders. None of these approaches requires major overhaul or structural changes but rather they just tinker with the way in which activities are being performed.

Structural change and renewal

A common problem that generates decline is the decreasing rate of variation and change that comes with aging. Thus, what once might have been a source of competitive advantage can turn into a lock-in and hamper change. Addressing this issue can require structural change so that an industry, a cluster, or a company can reboot itself. This would mean creating variety in the form of new business models, innovations, or companies that are able to match changing conditions. This variation can then help get rid of lock-in and generate renewal.

In practice, structural change can take place in several ways. First, structural change can happen organically without the influence of a third party. For instance, incumbent firms within an industry can be replaced by more specialized companies that are better suited to changing conditions (Fasenfest and Jacobs 2003). However, structural change also often requires an external intervention. Therefore, the second way to instigate change is to create infrastructure such as universities and R&D intensive organizations, or directly attract new firms through infrastructure investments. These actions create variety in terms of innovation and the kind of companies that operate in a locale. A third option is to develop supporting ecosystems and organizations, or introduce public support mechanisms that facilitate transformation from the old to the new. These actions can help companies to carve a new path of growth.

Letting go at the point of no return

While we noted earlier that any industry, a cluster, or a company can be saved, it does not mean that they should be saved. In some instances, it is better to let go when an industry, a cluster, or a company has reached the point of no return. For instance, as the decline of the Mexican oil industry was caused by Mexico running out of oil (Haber, Maurer and Razo 2003), there is not much that can be done to remedy this situation. The extinction of industries, clusters, and companies is also necessary for the creation of something new since the struggle for survival is what fuels economic development. Thus, letting go should not be viewed as a failure but rather as a necessary action.

When a company is close to the point of no return, the logical way to manage decline is to let it happen and provide some form of terminal care: reducing the stigma of failure so that people can start anew or by disinvesting and milking assets as long as they have some worth. These actions can then dampen the effect of the expiration of an industry, a cluster, or a company. Letting go is also the most cost-efficient way of managing decline. Shareholders, taxpayers, and other sources of money and resources benefit from letting unsalvageable businesses to fail.

References

Adner, R., & Snow, D. (2010). Old technology responses to new technology threats: Demand heterogeneity and technology retreats. *Industrial and Corporate Change, 19*(5), 1655–1675. https://doi.org/10.1093/icc/dtq046

Arora, A., Branstetter, L. G., & Drev, M. (2013). Going soft: How the rise of software-based innovation led to the decline of Japan's IT industry and the resurgence of Silicon Valley. *Review of Economics and Statistics, 95*(3), 757–775. https://doi.org/10.1162/REST_a_00286

Braguinsky, S., & Hounshell, D. A. (2016). History and nanoeconomics in strategy and industry evolution research: Lessons from the Meiji-Era Japanese cotton spinning industry. *Strategic Management Journal, 37*(1), 45–65. https://doi.org/10.1002/smj.2452

Cameron, K. S., Sutton, R. I., & Whetten, D. A. (1988). *Readings in Organizational Decline: Frameworks, Research, and Prescriptions.* Cambridge: Ballinger.

Chandler, G. N., Broberg, J. C., & Allison, T. H. (2014). Customer value propositions in declining industries: Differences between industry representative and high-growth firms. *Strategic Entrepreneurship Journal, 8*(3), 234–253. https://doi.org/10.1002/sej.1181

Dalum, B., Pedersen, C. Ø., & Villumsen, G. (2005). Technological life-cycles: Lessons from a cluster facing disruption. *European Urban and Regional Studies, 12*(3), 229–246. https://doi.org/10.1177/0969776405056594

De Propris, L., & Lazzeretti, L. (2009). Measuring the decline of a Marshallian industrial district: The Birmingham jewellery quarter. *Regional Studies*, *43*(9), 1135–1154. https://doi.org/10.1080/00343400802070894

Donnelly, T., Begley, J., & Collis, C. (2017). The West Midlands automotive industry: The road downhill. *Business History*, *59*(1), 56–74. https://doi.org/10.1080/0 0076791.2016.1235559

Fasenfest, D., & Jacobs, J. (2003). An anatomy of change and transition: The automobile industry of Southeast Michigan. *Small Business Economics*, *21*(2), 153–172. https://doi.org/10.1023/A:1025018626406

Freedman, C., & Blair, A. (2010). Seeds of destruction: The decline and fall of the US car industry. *The Economic and Labour Relations Review*, *21*(1), 105–126. https://doi.org/10.1177/103530461002100109

Haber, S., Maurer, N., & Razo, A. (2003). When the law does not matter: The rise and decline of the Mexican oil industry. *The Journal of Economic History*, *63*(1), 1–32. https://doi.org/10.1017/S0022050703001712

Hannigan, T. J., Cano-Kollmann, M., & Mudambi, R. (2015). Thriving innovation amidst manufacturing decline: The Detroit auto cluster and the resilience of local knowledge production. *Industrial and Corporate Change*, *24*(3), 613–634. https://doi.org/10.1093/icc/dtv014

Harrigan, K. R., & Porter, M. E. (1983). End-game strategies for declining industries. *Harvard Business Review*, *61*(4), 111–120.

Kalafsky, R. V., & MacPherson, A. D. (2002). The competitive characteristics of US manufacturers in the machine tool industry. *Small Business Economics*, *19*(4), 355–369. https://doi.org/10.1023/A:1019676202588

Karniouchina, E. V., Carson, S. J., Short, J. C., & Ketchen Jr, D. J. (2013). Extending the firm vs. industry debate: Does industry life cycle stage matter? *Strategic Management Journal*, *34*(8), 1010–1018. https://doi.org/10.1002/smj.2042

Kimberly, J. R., & Miles, R. H. (Eds.). (1980). *The Organizational Life Cycle: Issues in the Creation, Transformation and Decline of Organizations*. San Francisco: Jossey-Bass Inc.

Klepper, S. (1997). Industry life cycles. *Industrial and Corporate Change*, *6*(1), 145–182. https://doi.org/10.1093/icc/6.1.145

Klepper, S. (2016). *Experimental Capitalism: The Nanoeconomics of American High-Tech Industries*. Princeton: Princeton University Press.

Kuilman, J. G., & van Driel, H. (2013). You too, Brutus? Category demise in Rotterdam warehousing, 1871–2011. *Industrial and Corporate Change*, *22*(2), 511–548. https://doi.org/10.1093/icc/dts019

Lamberg, J. A., Lubinaitė, S., Ojala, J., & Tikkanen, H. (2021). The curse of agility: The Nokia Corporation and the loss of market dominance in mobile phones, 2003–2013. *Business History*, *63*(4), 574–605. https://doi.org/10.1080/00076791 .2019.1593964

Lamberg, J. A., & Peltoniemi, M. (2020). The nanoeconomics of firm-level decision-making and industry evolution: Evidence from 200 years of paper and pulp making. *Strategic Management Journal*, *41*(3), 499–529. https://doi.org/10.1002/smj.3080

Lazonick, W. (1981). Competition, specialization, and industrial decline. *Journal of Economic History*, 31–38.

Lazonick, W. (1983). Industrial organization and technological change: The decline of the British cotton industry. *Business History Review*, *57*(2), 195–236. https://doi.org/10.2307/3114355

Leonard-Barton, D. (1992). Core capabilities and core rigidities: A paradox in managing new product development. *Strategic Management Journal*, *13*(S1), 111–125. https://doi.org/10.1002/smj.4250131009

Menzel, M. P., & Fornahl, D. (2010). Cluster life cycles – Dimensions and rationales of cluster evolution. *Industrial and Corporate Change*, *19*(1), 205–238. https://doi.org/10.1093/icc/dtp036

Miles, G., Snow, C. C., & Sharfman, M. P. (1993). Industry variety and performance. *Strategic Management Journal*, *14*(3), 163–177. https://doi.org/10.1002/smj.4250140302

Mudambi, R., Mudambi, S. M., Mukherjee, D., & Scalera, V. G. (2017). Global connectivity and the evolution of industrial clusters: From tires to polymers in Northeast Ohio. *Industrial Marketing Management*, *61*(1), 20–29. https://doi.org/10.1016/j.indmarman.2016.07.007

Vernon, R. (1966). International investment and international trade in the product cycle. *Quarterly Journal of Economics*, *80*(2), 190–207. https://doi.org/10.1016/B978-0-12-444281-8.50024-6

Zammuto, R. F., & Cameron, K. S. (1982). Environmental decline and organizational response. *Academy of Management Proceedings*, *1982*(1), pp. 250–254. Briarcliff Manor: Academy of Management. https://doi.org/10.5465/ambpp.1982.4976626

Index

Note: Page numbers in *italics* indicate figures and page numbers in **bold** indicate tables on the corresponding page.